Th

FOCUS ENGLISH

BOOK 1

BILL RIDGWAY

EDWARD ARNOLD

About Focused English

Ashfold is a town somewhere in this country. It is a make-believe town, with make-believe people living in make-believe houses in make-believe streets. But Ashfold is just like a real town. It could be *your* town, or the town near your home.

Ashfold has stores and factories, buses and trains, old houses and new estates, a police station, a fire brigade and a hospital. There are dances for the old and discos for the young. There are children and babies and men and women and most of them live in families just like yours.

The exercises in this book are all about Ashfold. They are quite easy to do, and there are drawings you can copy if you wish. When you've finished the book, you may notice the different things to look at in the place where *you* live. Things you've never really thought about before.

This book can be used in your English lessons. The book which runs along with it is called *Focused Maths*. It's also about Ashfold, but this time it's the Maths that's important – and you'll find it just as easy to do.

I hope you enjoy yourself.

First published in Great Britain 1985
by Edward Arnold (Publishers) Ltd
41 Bedford Square
London WC1B 3DQ

Edward Arnold (Australia) Pty Ltd
80 Waverley Road
Caulfield East
Victoria 3145
Australia

Drawings by Tony Hargreaves and Brian Lythgoe

British Library Cataloguing in Publication Data

Ridgway, Bill
Focused English 1.
1. English language—Examinations, questions, etc.
I. Title
428.2 PE1112

ISBN 0 7131 7452 8

Set in 12/13 Univers by DP Press, Sevenoaks
Printed by Thomson Litho Ltd, East Kilbride, Scotland

Contents

1 Ashfold

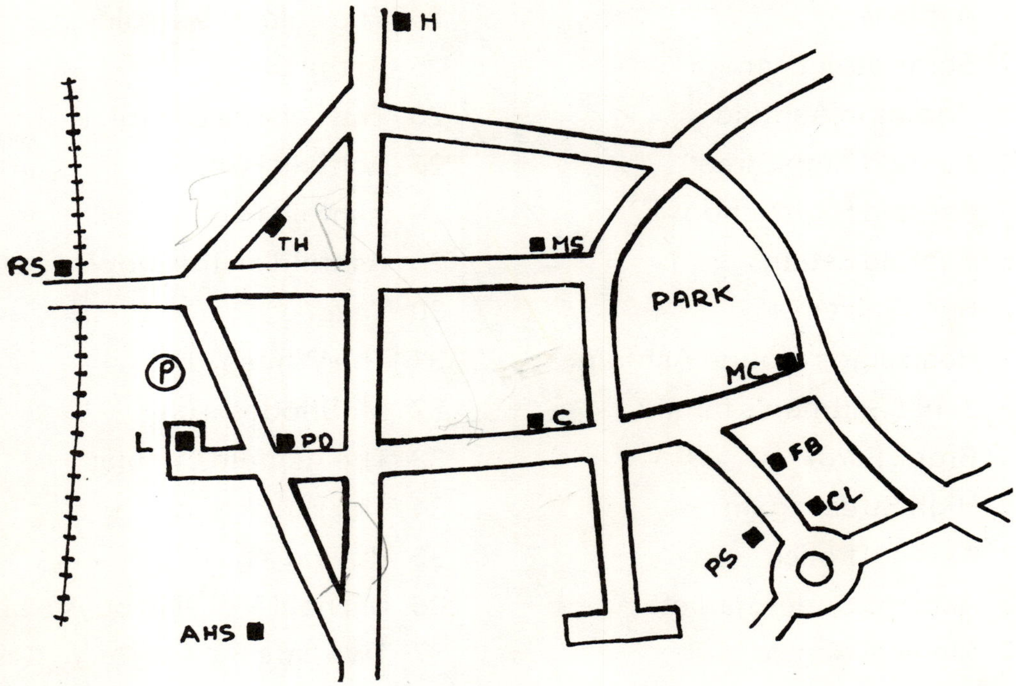

This is a map of Ashfold. The black boxes are the main places.

H is HOSPITAL. MS is MIDDLE SCHOOL.

1 Write down what you think these are:

RS (you get a train here)
PO (you get a stamp here)
PS (you get the police here)
L (you get books here)
C (you see a film here)
FB (you send for them if there's a fire)

2 Write letters for:

Town Hall Clinic Car Park Ashfold High School Medical Centre

You walk from the Police Station to the Railway Station. Name the places you pass.

2 Some street names

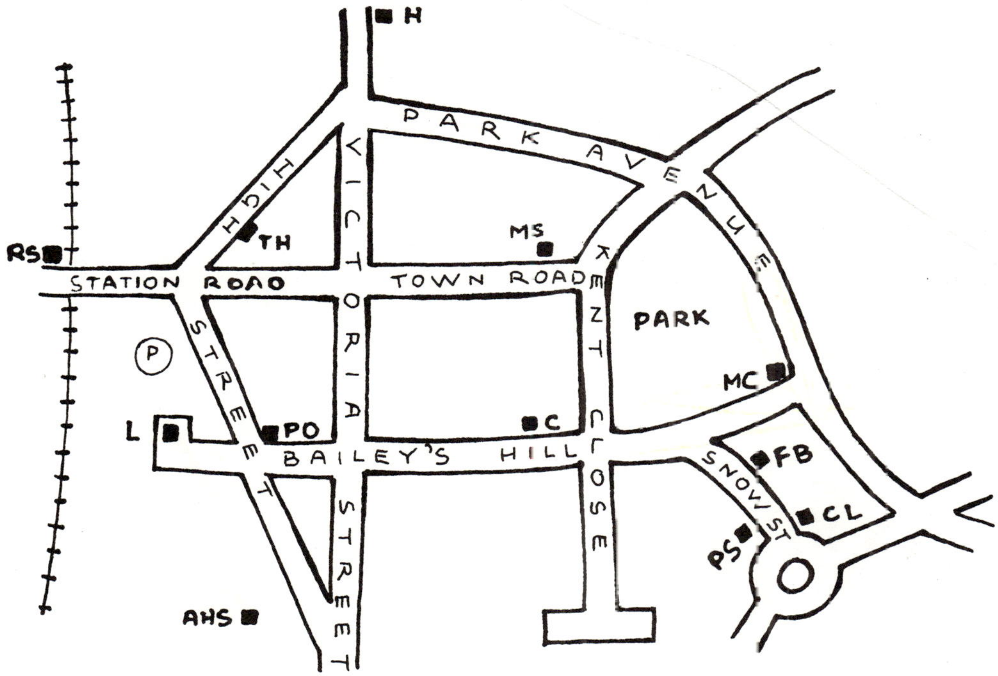

This is a map of Ashfold. It shows the main roads and streets.

1 Which street is the Town Hall (TH) on?

2 Which street is the Fire Brigade (FB) on?

3 Which road is the Railway Station (RS) on?

4 Which road is the Cinema (C) on?

5 Name the place on the corner of High Street and Bailey's Hill.

6 Name the place on the corner of Park Avenue and Bailey's Hill.

7 Name the place on the other side of the road from the Clinic (CL).

8 Name a street that would take me from the Hospital (H) to Ashfold High School (AHS).

9 Name two roads that go from the Railway Station (RS) to the Middle School (MS).

Copy the map. Leave out street names. Put in the places.

3 Homes in Ashfold

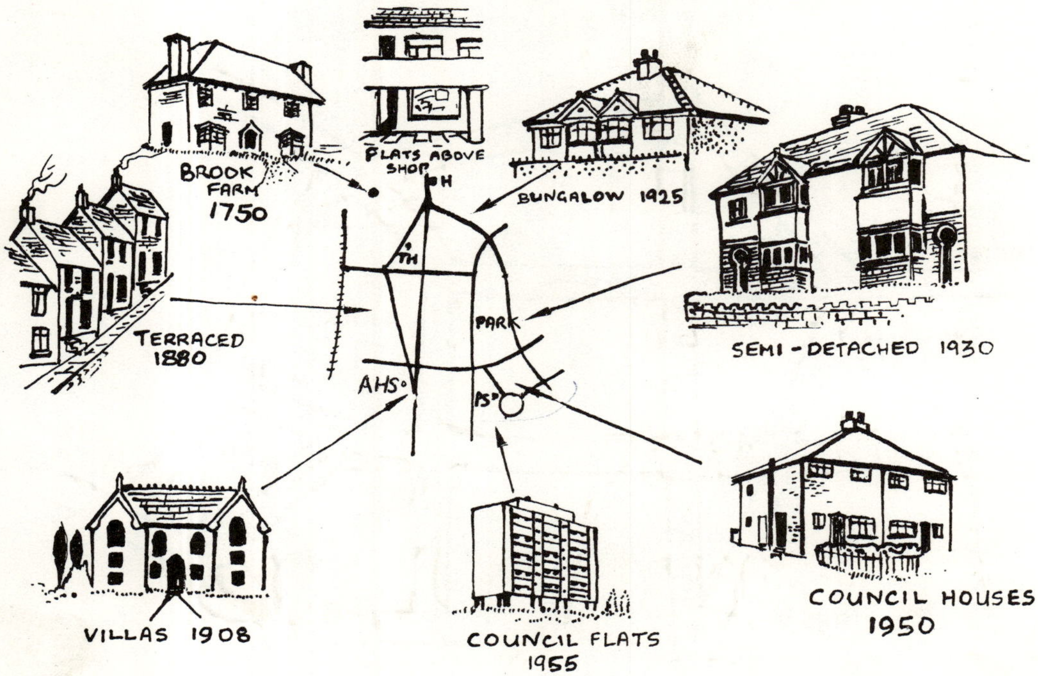

1. When was Brook Farm built?
2. When was the bungalow built?
3. When were the villas built?
4. What is the oldest building shown?
5. What was built first – the council houses or the council flats?
6. What kind of houses are near the High School (AHS)?
7. Which is older – the terraced houses or the semi-detached houses?
8. How many years was it between the building of the terraced houses and the building of the villas?

Look at chapter 2

9. On which street would you find the semi-detached houses?
10. Name the street where you would find council houses.

Draw your own house.
Write down what sort of house it is (e.g. council house).

4 Ashfold High Street

Baker	Fish · Chips
HARDWARE	BANK
Supermarket	WOOLWORTH
DECORATOR	Rose & Crown
CHEMIST	GARAGE

These are some of the words you would see in Ashfold High Street.

1 Write the name of the pub.
2 Write the name of the place that mends cars.
3 Write the name of the place where you get money.
4 Write the name of the shop that sells bread and cakes.
5 Where do you get pills from?
6 Where can you get a hot meal from?
7 Name the big store that sells food.
8 Name the big store that doesn't sell food.
9 Write the name of the paint and wallpaper shop.
10 A hard______ shop sells nails and tools. Write down the full word.

Write down five other words you might find in Ashfold High Street.

5 Ashfold High School

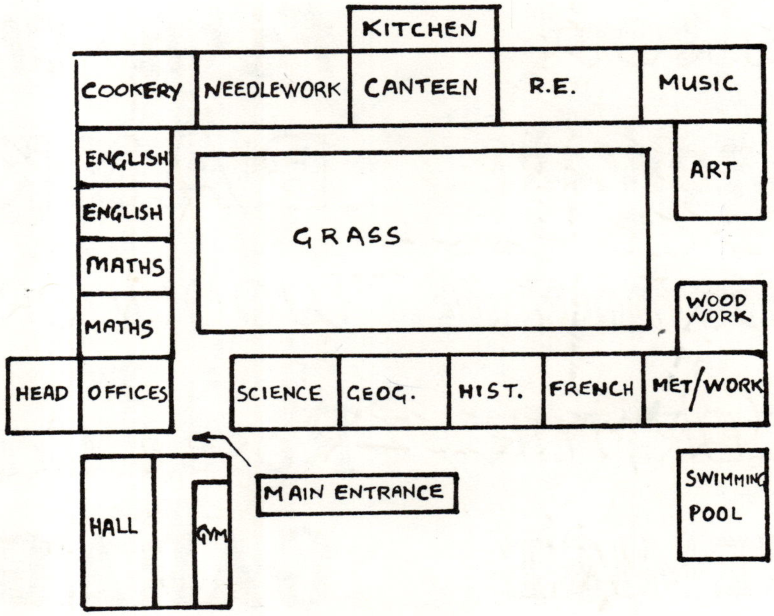

This is a plan of Ashfold High School.

1 In how many rooms is English taught?

2 In how many rooms is Maths taught?

3 What subject is taught in the room next to Art?

4 What subject do you think is taught in the room next to Woodwork?

5 What other room can be found in the Hall block?

6 What three subjects are taught between Science and Metalwork?

7 What room do you go through if you want to see the Head?

8 Name the subjects taught on each side of the Canteen.

9 Which subject-rooms would you pass if you wanted to walk from the Canteen to the Swimming Pool?

Write any subjects you do at your school that are not shown on the plan of Ashfold High School.

6 Ashfold Estate

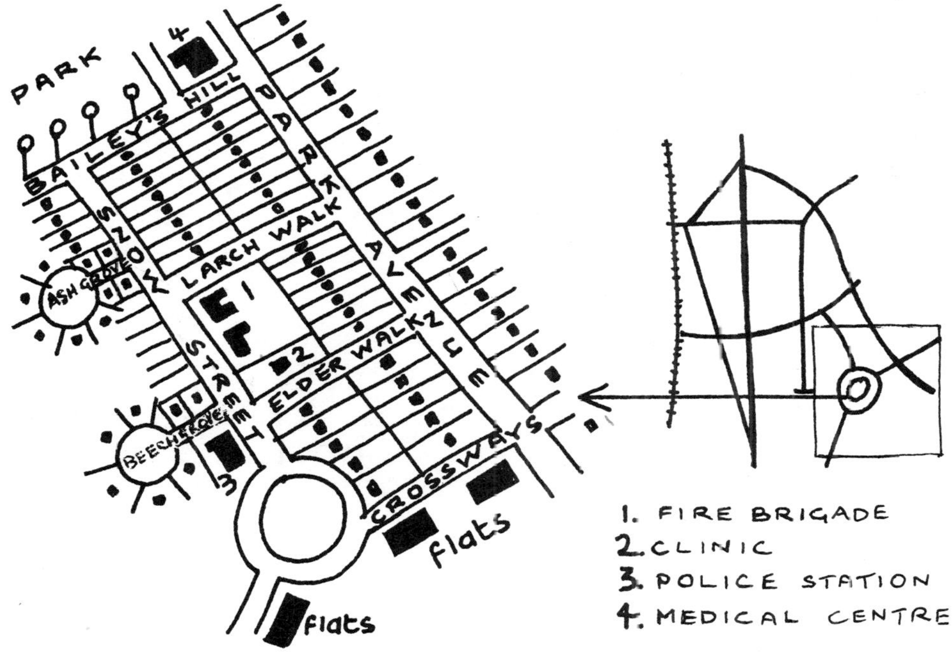

Copy the writing. Put words from the box into the gaps.

Ashfold ______ is a big place. It is a ______ estate. There are houses and ______. There is a clinic, a ______ Station, a ______ Brigade and a Medical Centre. There are only a few shops. The main streets are Bailey's ______, Snow Street and Park Avenue. Ash ______ and ______ Grove are cul-de-sacs. They are dead-ends.

flats	**Grove**	**estate**	**council**
Police	**Hill**	**Beech**	**Fire**

Draw a simple plan to show where *you* live.
Write the streets you know on your plan.

7 Ben Walker

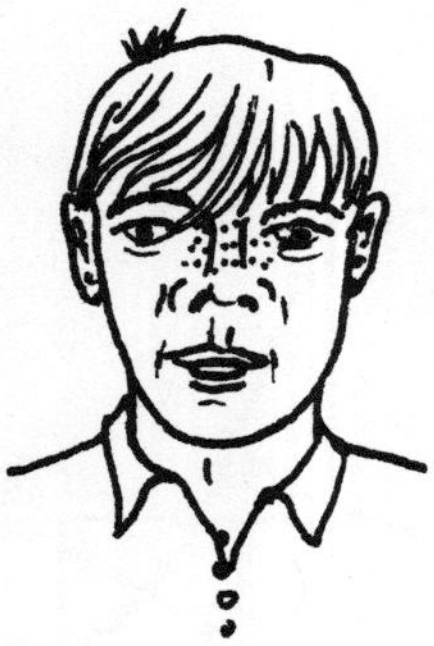

Ben Walker lives on Ashfold Estate. His address is 6, Snow Street. He is 14. He has a brother called Rob. Rob is only 6 months old. His mother is named Eth, and his father is Jack. Eth had a part time job on the mill. She was laid off last summer. Jack used to be a miner. He got hurt down the pit. Now he's unemployed. Ben goes to Ashfold High School. He has a part time job on the market stalls.

1 How old is Ben?
2 How old is Rob?
3 What is Ben's mother named?
4 What is his father called?
5 Where does Ben go to school?
6 What is Ben's part time job?
7 What did Jack Walker used to be?
8 Where did Eth used to work?
9 When did Eth lose her job?
10 How many are there in the family?
11 Write the word which means 'out of work'.
12 Write a word meaning 'coal-mine'.

Write about your family and where you live.
Write what your father and mother do.

8 Road signs around Ashfold

1 There is a GIVE WAY AHEAD sign at the end of Park Avenue. Copy the sign.

2 There is a PARKING PLACE sign near the library. Copy the sign. Colour the shaded part blue.

3 There are LIMITED WAITING signs on Victoria Street. The words are white. What colour is the rest of the sign, do you think?

4 Copy the SCHOOL KEEP CLEAR sign. There is one outside Ashfold Middle School.

5 There is a NO RIGHT TURN sign at the top of the High Street. Copy the sign. Colour the shaded part black.

6 Draw the TOILETS sign. There is a toilet in Ashfold car park.

Can you think of any other signs you might see in Ashfold?
Draw some.

9 Janet Saltman's family

The Saltman family live at Brook Farm, near the railway.

	NAME	AGE	JOB	
	Gordon	34	Farmer	married
	Jane	36	Housewife	
	Gran	64	Housewife	married
	Grandad	65	Retired farmer	

There are 4 children. Sid(7) and Eliot(5) go to Ashfold Middle and Infant school. Mike(3) is at home. Janet(11) has just started at Ashfold High School.

Answer TRUE or FALSE.

1 Grandad Saltman is 65.
2 Mrs Jane Saltman is 36.
3 Gordon and Jane Saltman have six children.
4 Sid is 5 and Eliot is 7.
5 Janet goes to Ashfold High School.
6 Gran goes to Ashfold High School.
7 Gordon is two years younger than Jane.
8 Grandad is a year younger than Gran.
9 Mike is at home.
10 Eliot goes to Ashfold Middle and Infant School.
11 Grandad was a farmer.
12 Gran is an astronaut.

Write down the name and age of the people in your family.

10 Brook Farm

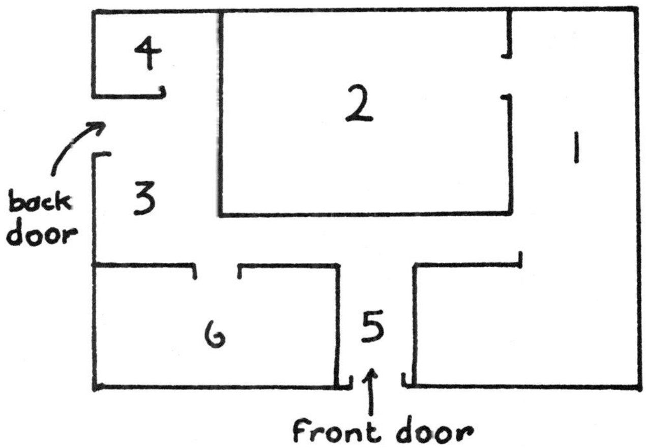

Here is a plan of the downstairs rooms at Brook Farm.

1 Copy the plan. Make it big. Miss out the numbers.
2 Write LIVING ROOM where it says 1.
3 Write KITCHEN where it says 6.
4 Write STORE where it says 4.
5 Write SITTING ROOM where it says 2.
6 Write HALL where it says 5.
7 Write DINING ROOM where it says 3.
8 Which room do you go through to get to the sitting room?
9 Which room is between the kitchen and the store?
10 Which room does the back door lead into?
11 Draw the farmhouse.

Draw a plan of your flat or bungalow. If you live in a house, do a plan of the downstairs part.

11 High Street again

This is Ashfold High Street on Saturday morning.

Copy the boxes opposite and tick YES or NO.

		YES	NO
1	Can you see a bus in the picture?	✓	
2	Can you see an aeroplane?		
3	Is there a bank?		
4	Is there an offer on at the supermarket?		
5	Is there somewhere to post a letter?		
6	Is there somewhere to buy a gas cooker?		
7	Is there a lorry in the picture?		
8	Are some of the windows dirty?		
9	Can you see a helicopter?		
10	Is the policeman holding a walkie-talkie?		
11	Can you see a baby in the pram?		

Draw a busy High Street near where you live.

12 Ashfold Police

1

2

3

4

5

Copy this out.
Use words from the box to fill the gaps.

The Police ______ at Ashfold is between Beech Grove and Snow ______. It is on Ashfold ______. Ashfold is a big town. The police are always ______.

busy Station Estate Street

Match the picture-number with the words:

11.00 p.m. There's a fight near the Rose and Crown.	3
8.30 a.m. There has been a bad car crash.	
12.30 p.m. This man has been driving while drunk.	
4.30 p.m. He has been riding too fast.	
3.00 p.m. She's stealing from a supermarket.	

13 Ashfold Supermarket

Here are eight things you can buy from the supermarket at Ashfold.

1. Tea is sold in packets. What is coffee sold in?
2. What is paint sold in?
3. What is wine sold in?
4. What is toothpaste sold in?
5. What are sold in bunches?
6. What are sold in packs?
7. How many things cost less than £1?
8. How many things cost £2 or more?
9. Which things have a top you screw off?
10. Which thing has a lid you can get off with a screw-driver?

Ashfold Supermarket sells many more things.
Draw a picture-chart of eight other things you think you can buy.
Make it like the one at the top of this page.

14 Medical Centre

Fill in the gaps:

Ashfold Medical Centre is between ______ Avenue and ______ Hill.

Look at the plan of Ashfold Medical Centre. Name these people:

1 He wears glasses and has a beard.
2 He is bald and wears glasses.
3 He is bald, has a beard and does not wear glasses.
4 She is dark-haired and wears long ear-rings. She is not a doctor.
5 He has no beard, dark hair and does not wear glasses. He is not a doctor.
6 He has a round face and a tie with dots on it. He is always smiling.
7 She has short, fair hair. Her room is next to Dr Jones's room.
8 He has a thin face and bushy eyebrows. His room is next to the entrance.

15 Michael McLeish

Michael McLeish is 12. He lives in the flats at Crossways. The Police Station is near. If he goes up Park Avenue he can go to the Medical Centre and Ashfold Park.

Michael's mum is Doreen. She is divorced. She works in an office. His dad lives away. His grandad lives with them. He's his mother's father. His name is Bill.

Copy and tick the TRUE or FALSE part.

		TRUE	FALSE
1	Michael McLeish is 12.	✓	
2	He lives in the flats.		
3	The flats are at Crossfields.		
4	The Police Station is miles away.		
5	His mum's name is Pam.		
6	She works in a shop.		
7	His dad lives away.		
8	His grandmother lives with them.		
9	Grandad's name is Bill.		
10	He is the father of Doreen McLeish.		
11	Michael looks happy in the picture.		

How is a flat different from a house?
Can you give three differences?

16 Ashfold Garage

Copy the words and fill in the gaps with words from the box.

This is Ashfold ______ . It is aways ______ . They sell ______ outside and ______ them inside.

The picture shows a car being mended. It is on a ______ . A ______ is doing something under the car. Another mechanic is working with him. On the ______ are ______ and ______ . On the wall behind the bench are some ______ .

There is a ______ shining under the car. There are two spare ______ on the shelf at the back.

busy mechanic ramp tins cars bench
mend tools lamp tyres garage bottles

Make a list of the other things you can see in the picture.
Draw the picture.

17 Shop signs

Match the eight signs you see in Ashfold High Street with the eight sentences.

1 This shop sells all the stuff you need for fishing. (F)
2 This shop sells paint and wallpaper. It is a decorator's.
3 This shop sells flowers. It is a florist's.
4 You get your eyes tested here. It is an optician's.
5 You can eat here. This is a restaurant.
6 This is a stationer's. You buy pens, pencils and paper here.
7 This striped pole is a hairdresser's sign.
8 You can buy bread and cakes here, at the baker's.

Think of signs for a butcher's, a garage and the Rose and Crown pub. Draw each sign. Colour it in.

18 Ashfold Library

The books in Ashfold Library are about all kinds of things. The six boxes show some of them.

Match the six people with the six boxes.

1	HISTORY
2	TRAVEL
3	FICTION
4	GARDENING
5	BUILDING
6	LANGUAGES

19 Open-Air Market

There is an open-air market on Ashfold car park each Wednesday.

Look at the numbers below. Write TRUE or FALSE for each one.

		TRUE	FALSE
1	Edwards' stall sells rolls of cloth.	✓	
2	Smith's stall sells groceries.		
3	There is a rabbit near the potatoes.		
4	Five birds are pecking at a worm.		
5	One stall sells shoes.		
6	Boots are hanging from the top.		
7	The woman with the little girl is by the shoe stall.		
8	There are two sacks of potatoes.		
9	One of the pot plants has been knocked over.		
10	Only one pot plant is standing.		
11	A man is selling groceries.		

List 10 things you can get at an open-air market.

20 Mary Wong

Mary Wong is 11. She lives with her mother and father and her two sisters in a flat above the fish and chip shop. Her dad is from Hong Kong. He bought the shop 6 years ago. His name is Wy. Her mum is from Ashfold. Her name is Susan. Mary's sisters are Sally and Wendy. They are twins. They are 8 years old.

Answer YES or NO:

1 Does Mary have a brother?
2 Is Mary the oldest sister?
3 Do the Wong Family live in a flat?
4 Does Wy Wong come from Hong Kong?
5 Is Mrs Wong's name Susan?
6 Do the Wong family run a sweet shop?
7 Are Sally and Wendy twins?
8 Are Sally and Wendy five years old?
9 Is Mrs Wong from Ashfold?
10 Is Mary Wong 11?
11 Is Mary three years older than Sally?

Draw a plan of Mary Wong's flat. There will be a kitchen, a bathroom and three bedrooms.

21 Menu

Cod	55p	Peas	18p
Plaice	52p	Meat & Potato Pie	30p
Chips	25p	Steak & Kidney Pie	32p
Small sausage	9p	Chicken	70p
Jumbo sausage	18p	Scampi	99p

You can get a cheap take-away meal at Wong's. Their prices are good. Their fish and chips are better.

Copy the sentences below. Fill in the gaps with words from the menu.

1 I'd like Cod and ______ please.
2 I'd like ______ and chips please.
3 Could I have chips and two small ______ please?
4 Could I have a Jumbo ______ please?
5 A ______, chips and ______ please.
6 Do you have a ______ and potato pie?
7 We have no more ______ and kidney pies. Will a meat and ______ pie be okay?
8 Chicken and ______ please. Three times.
9 Could I have a ______, a carton of ______ and a Jumbo ______ please?

Choose a meal for yourself from the things on the menu.

22 Ashfold at play

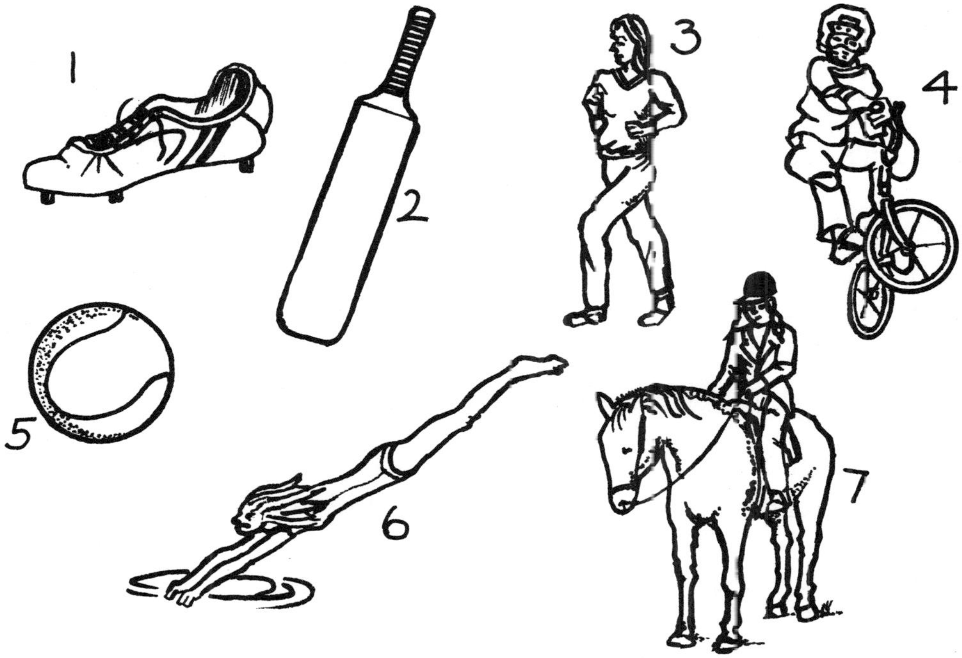

There are all sorts of sports and games you can play in Ashfold.

Match the pictures with the people. Begin like this – **A7**

A Janet Saltman likes riding her horse around her dad's farm.

B Ben Walker enjoys cricket in the summer.

C Michael McLeish is a football fan. He's a fan of Ashfold FC.

D Mary Wong has a BMX bike. She enjoys racing.

E Linda Klosowski goes to the baths every week.

F Jill White likes jogging.

G Toby Rhodes plays tennis with his sister.

Here is a sentence about jogging:

Jogging helps to keep you fit.

Write sentences about three other sports. Draw pictures.

23 Ashfold Baths

Ashfold Baths is part of the Leisure Centre. There are 2 pools. There is a big one for people who can swim and a small one for those who are learning. Ashfold Baths is open 7 days a week. It is open on a Monday night, Wednesday night, Friday night and Saturday night.
You can join a swimming club, and an under-water club. You can also get your bronze, silver and gold medals and your Life-Saving Certificate. You pay 70p a time at the Swimming Club. There is a coffee and sweets machine at the baths. And there is a place where you can buy arm-bands and flippers.

1 How many pools are there at Ashfold Baths?

2 Who is the small pool for?

3 Write down the **nights** Ashfold Baths is open.

4 What medals can you get?

5 What certificate can you get?

6 How much is it for the Swimming Club?

7 What can you get from the coffee machine besides coffee?

8 What can you get from the sweets machine?

9 What else can you get besides arm-bands and flippers for swimming?

10 Draw the skin-diver.

Why is it a good thing to be able to swim?
Can *you* swim? How old were you when you learnt?

24 The Palace, Ashfold

1 What film is showing on SCREEN 1?

2 What film is showing on SCREEN 2?

3 What is the name of the LATE MOVIE?

4 What time does CHILD OF THE ZOMBIE start?

5 How many times a day is SWORDFISH PATROL showing?

6 When is the first time SWORDFISH PATROL is showing?

7 When is the last time?

8 How many times a day is SPACE ACE showing?

9 If I went to see SPACE ACE just after tea, at what time would I have to be at THE PALACE?

10 I go to see the film on SCREEN 2. I get there at 8.10 pm. How much have I missed?

Copy the board which shows what's on at THE PALACE.
Write your own film names instead of the names given.

25 At the Disco

There is a disco at Ashfold Town Hall every Friday. It starts at 7.30 and goes on until 12. It costs £1 to go in. The D.J. is Dave Brown. He lives at Wint. It's about 3 miles from Ashfold. He has a van and a record deck. He's put lights around the deck to make it look good. He always buys the latest chart singles, but he has old records too. There is a bar and tables where you can stand and have a drink.

Copy the writing. Fill in the gaps with words from the box.

There is a ______ at the Town ______ on ______ .

Dave ______ is the name of the ______ . The dance goes on until ______ .

You can stand at a ______ and have a ______ . Dave has most of the latest ______ , and when he plays them the lights go on and off.

Hall Fridays disco D.J. 12 Brown
drink table singles

Have you ever been to a dance or a disco?
Where was it? Write about it.

26 The Leisure Centre

SQUASH FIRST AID OFFICE

REFRESHMENTS STORES SHOWERS

SWIMMING POOL RIFLE RANGE

BASKETBALL CHANGING ROOMS

Here are some of the words you could see if you went to the Ashfold Leisure Centre.

These are the same words, mixed up. Copy them out correctly.

1 offcie (office)
2 shersow
3 frist adi
4 stroes
5 refershemnts
6 chagning oorms
7 smmingwi oolp
8 rflie rnage
9 ketlabbasl
10 quashs

Write down 2 ball games.
Where would you go to fire at a target?
Are there any other words you may find at the Leisure Centre?
If you can think of some, put them down.

27 Ashfold Park

A

B

C

D

E

F

Here are some of the things you can do in Ashfold Park.

Match the picture with the words:

1 On Sunday afternoons the band plays.

2 Some people play bowls.

3 There is somewhere for the children to enjoy themselves.

4 Some people like fishing in the park lake.

5 Many flowers are grown in the greenhouses.

6 You can hire a boat for £1 an hour.

Is there anything else to do in the park?
What?

28 Ashfold FC

Ashfold Football Club is near the Park. It takes about 15 minutes to walk there from the Town Centre. It was started in 1875. The ground is not very big. When the team is playing at home you get about 3000 there. The team's not very well up in the league. That doesn't please a lot of people. Half Ashfold's football mad. A lot of money was spent on the ground last year. Now they're in the red trying to pay for it.

1. Where is Ashfold Football Club?
2. How long does it take to walk there from the Town Centre?
3. When was it started?
4. How many do you get at the ground when the team is playing at home?
5. Is the team well up in the league?
6. Do many people in Ashfold like football?
7. What was the money spent on last year?
8. What does 'in the red' mean?
9. Why is Ashfold FC in the red?
10. What sort of things were done to the ground, do you think?

Write a few sentences about your nearest football club.

29 Ashfold on the move

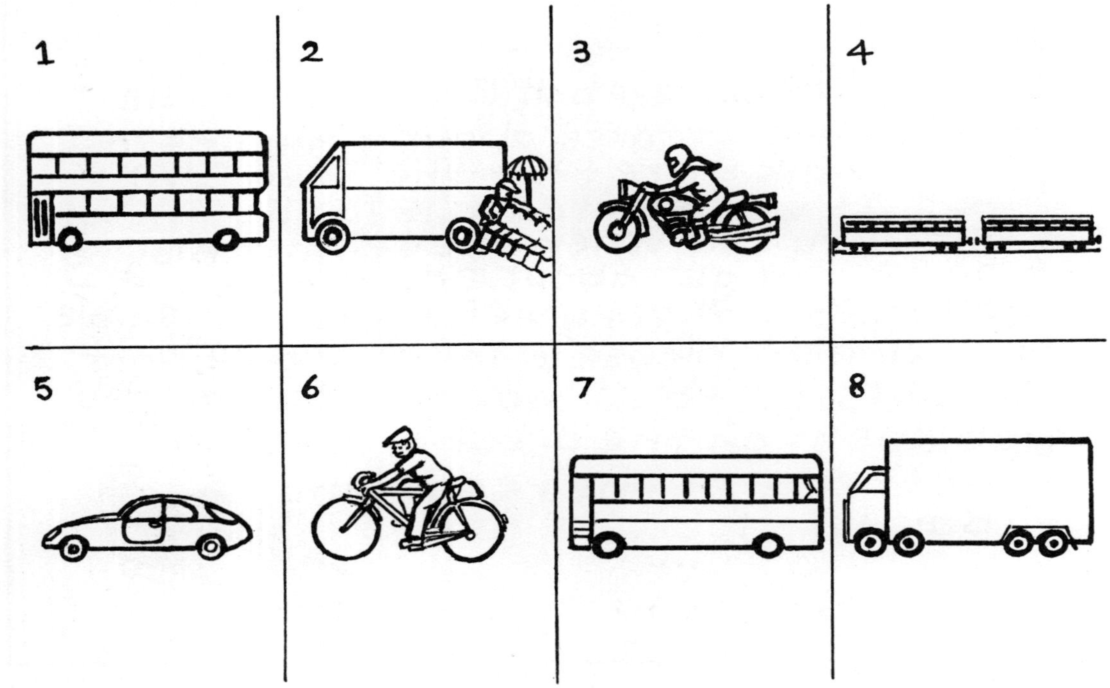

These are some of the ways you can move around Ashfold.

Put picture-numbers in the blanks

A This has two wheels and an engine. 3

B This has two wheels but no engine. ______

C This has eight wheels and brings goods to Ashfold. ______

D This has two decks and holds about 70 people. ______

E This has one deck and holds about 40 people. ______

F This stops at Ashfold Station. ______

G This holds furniture. ______

H A lot of people down your street might have one of these. ______

Make a list of any other kinds of transport you can see around town.

30 Taxi

Doreen McLeish sometimes drives a taxi for White's Taxis. She works in an office in the day, and her taxi-work is part-time at weekends or nights. Most of the people are all right. But she can get a bad fare from time to time. It's worse when the pubs close. White's Taxis are all painted red. They are mainly Ladas because Ladas are cheap and roomy. The longer the trip, the more you pay. There is a meter fixed to the front. The meter shows the money you owe. Mrs McLeish doesn't like taxi-driving very much, but she has to do something to bring in extra money.

Fill in the blanks

1 Doreen McLeish works in the day in an o _ _ _ _ _ _ _ _ _ _ _ .

2 Doreen McLeish works part time for W _ _ _ _ _ _ _ _ _ _ _ T _ _ _ _ _ _ _ _ _ .

3 Sometimes she works at w _ _ _ _ _ _ _ _ _ _ _ _ _ _ _ .

4 She can get a bad fare when the _ _ _ _ _ s close.

5 Most of the t _ _ _ _ _ _ _ _ are L _ _ _ _ _ _ s.

6 Mr White buys L _ _ _ _ _ _ _ because they are ch _ _ _ _ _ and r _ _ _ my.

7 Mr White paints his taxis _ _ _ _ _ .

8 A m _ _ _ _ _ _ _ tells you how much money you owe.

9 Doreen Mc _ _ _ _ _ _ _ _ _ _ isn't very well off.

10 T _ _ _ _ _ _ _ are dearer than b _ _ s _ _ s.

Would *you* like to drive a taxi?
Why? Why not?

31 The Whites

Use what you know abcut the Whites to write this out in full.

The Whites are a family of four. There is Mr and Mrs White and two ______ . The son is named ______ and the girl is named ______ . Jill is ______ years older than Barry. Mr White is ______ years older than his ______ . Mr White has a good ______ business. He lives in a big house near Ashfold Park. Marj works part-time. She serves ____________ at Ashfold High School. Her daughter is in the second year there. She is clever. She is in the ______ class. Mrs White has always worn glasses. ______ takes after her.

What do you think the living room is like in the White's house?
Try and draw it.

32 Mr Rhodes's day

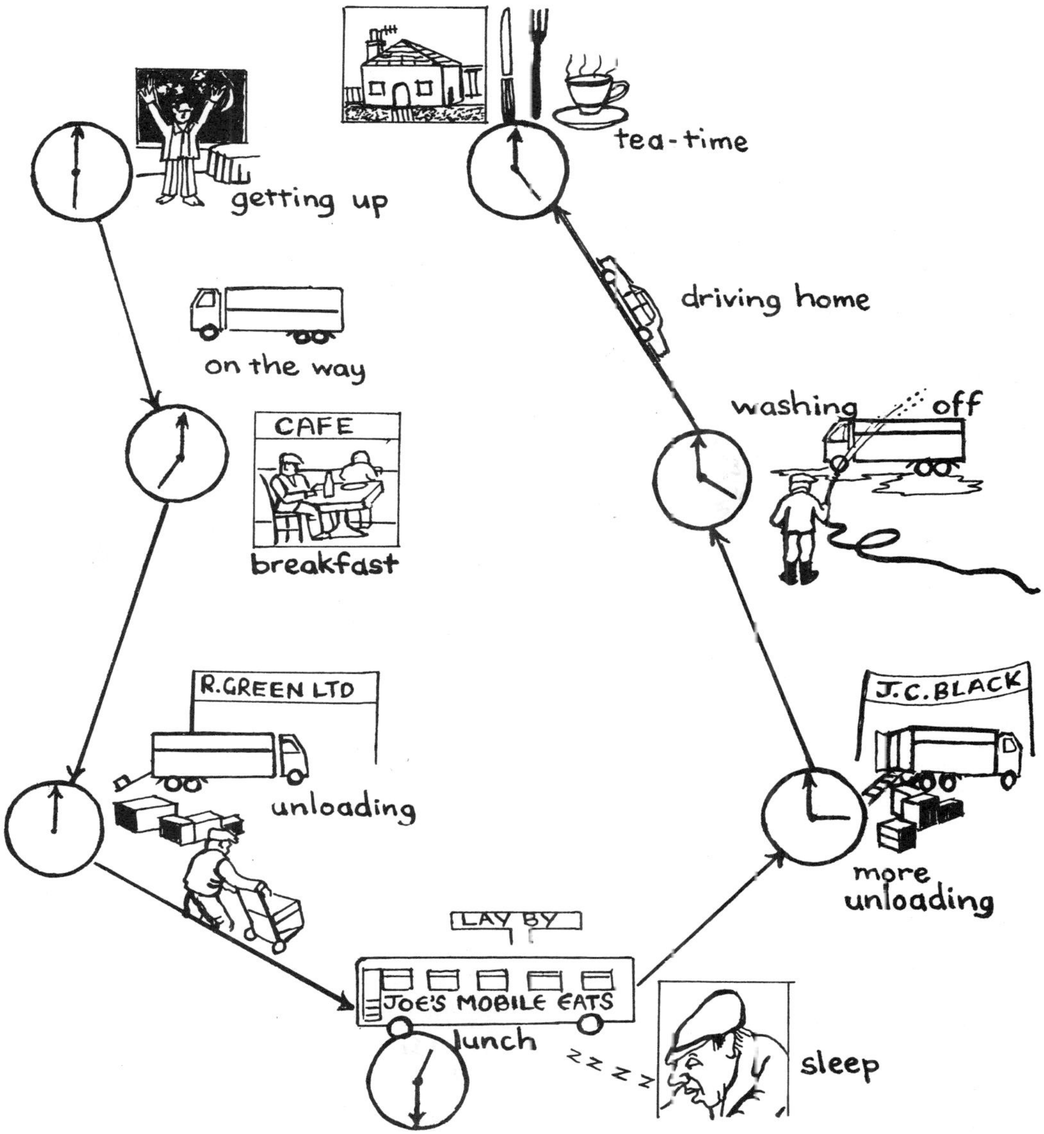

Mr Rhodes and his family live in a bungalow in Ashfold. He is a long-distance lorry driver. Sometimes he is away for a few days. But more often than not he can go there and back in a day.

Look at the plan of a day in the life of Mr Rhodes.
Write down what you think is happening.
Begin like this:

Mr Rhodes gets up at 6 o'clock and is soon on his way. At seven . . .

33 The Ashfold Circular

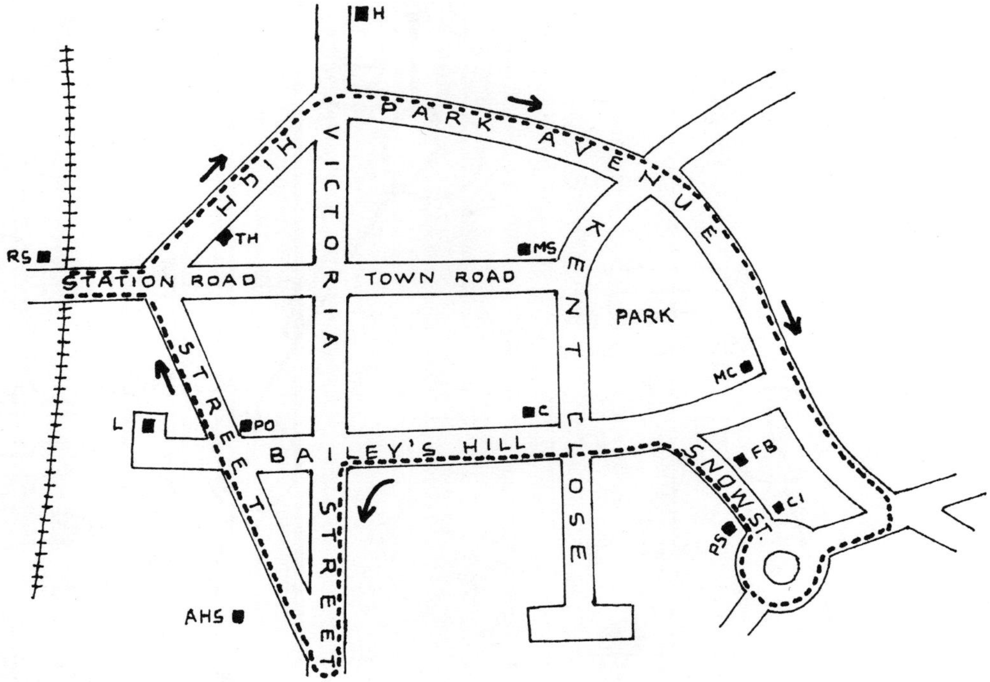

The Ashfold Circular is a bus-route around Ashfold. It starts at the station and ends at the station.

Answer YES or NO:

1. You live down Park Avenue. Does the bus go past your house?
2. You live in Snow Street. Does the bus go past your house?
3. You live in Town Road. Does the bus go past your house?
4. You want to go to the Medical Centre (MC). Does the bus go near it?
5. You want the Police Station (PS). Does the bus go near it?
6. You want the Middle School (MS). Does the bus go near it?
7. You want to go to the Town Hall. Does the bus go near it?
8. Does the bus go past the Hospital (H)?
9. Does the bus go down Kent Close?
10. Does the bus go round a roundabout?

34 The Wrights

Kevin Wright drives a bus on the Ashfold Circular. He has been a bus-driver for twenty years. Now he is 50. His wife is named Lisa. She is a year older than Mr. Wright. They have 3 sons and 2 daughters. The daughters are Candy and Mol. Candy is 10. Mol is 22. Mr. Wright got her a job in the office of the Ashfold Bus Company. Baz Wright is 16. He goes to Ashfold High. He is doing his C.S.E. exams this time. Dave goes to the Ashfold F.E. College. He is 18. Brian Wright is the oldest son. He is married and works in a car factory in the city. He is 27.

1 How old is Brian Wright?

2 How old is Lisa Wright?

3 How old is Baz Wright?

4 How much older than Candy is Mol?

5 How much younger than Dave is Baz?

6 How much older than Dave is Brian?

7 How old was Mr Wright when Candy was born?

8 How old was Mrs Wright when Brian was born?

9 How old was Mr Wright when he got a job on the buses?

10 Write the names and ages of all the Wright family, starting with the youngest and going up. Begin like this:

Candy 10
Baz 16

Mr Wright is a bus-driver. Write a few sentences about his day.

35 Buying a bike

	**RACER** 10 gears – very light – not very comfortable – centre pull brakes – good if you want to move fast
	**B.M.X.** no gears – very strong – will stand up to a lot of rough use – brakes – thick tyres to grip – not much good on a run – fast on dirt tracks or as a stunt bike
	**ROADSTER** 3 gears – strong – quite heavy – comfortable – side pull brakes – good for steady work around town shopping
	**TRICYCLE** no gears – strong – will stand a lot of wear and tear – made for younger children to ride in garden or along a safe path near home

These are some of the bikes that are sold in the bike shop at Ashfold.

1. Which bike would you choose if you wanted a fast 15-mile run in the country?
2. Which bike would be safe for your brother, aged 5?
3. Which bike would be best if you wanted a loaf of bread and a few tins from the local supermarket?
4. Which bike would you buy if you liked rough-riding and stunts in a place near your home?
5. Which bike would you choose for a comfortable ride around town?
6. Which bike would you choose if you lived in a hilly place and didn't mind the hard saddle?
7. Which bike would you choose for your little sister, if she couldn't ride a bike with two wheels?
8. Which bike would be best for short races around a bumpy track?

Choose one of the bikes in the picture. Say why you'd choose it.

36 Michael McLeish buys a bike

Michael McLeish's old bike is falling to bits. His mother says he takes no care of it. She tells him to stop riding it up and down kerbs when he's taking papers. He wants a new bike that will stand rough use. A bike he can have fun on at nights. He'd like a BMX but they cost at least £45 and that's a lot to pay. His mum says she'll pay £15 and his grandad says he'll pay £10. But Michael will have to pay the rest on H.P. out of his pocket-money and paper round.

Copy the box and tick YES or NO:

1 Does Michael McLeish have a part-time job?

2 Has Michael McLeish saved all the money he needs for a new bike?

3 Does he treat a bike gently?

4 Is his grandad kind?

5 Does Michael go out at night?

6 Does his mum think he should pay something himself?

7 Does Michael *only* have his papers-money to spend?

8 Do you think he will treat his new bike well if he gets one?

YES	NO

What do you think Michael's new bike will look like in a year? Draw a picture and write a few sentences.

37 Two cars

A lot of families in Ashfold have a car.
Here are two of them.

Jane Saltman's Car	Mr Grant White's Car

NAME	CITROEN 2CV6	JAGUAR XJ12
HOW OLD?	5 YEARS OLD	3 YEARS OLD
COST NEW	£2000	£14000
NOW WORTH	£350	£5000
POWER	650 c.c.	4000 c.c.
FUEL (in town)	46 m.p.g.	16 m.p.g.
TOP SPEED	70 m.p.h.	140 m.p.h.

Copy and tick the car part.

Citroen	Jag

1 This is a fast car.

2 This is the cheaper car.

3 This car has lost £9000 in three years.

4 This car has lost £1650 in five years.

5 This car is cheap to run.

6 This car is very powerful.

7 This car doesn't do many miles to the gallon. (m.p.g.)

8 This is the younger car.

9 This car is dear to buy, dear to run and the price drops quickly.

10 This car is cheap to buy, cheap to run, and the price drops slowly.

38 Filling Station

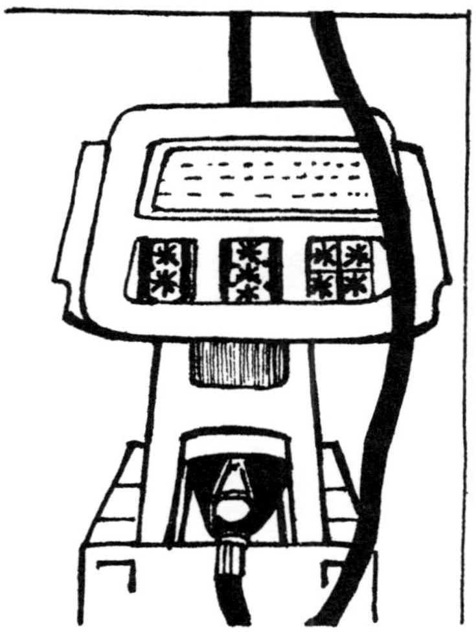

Instructions

1 Press the button to choose the grade.

2 Put the nozzle in the tank and fill.

3 Put the nozzle back.

4 Check the price. Pay for petrol.

There are three filling stations in Ashfold. They are all self-service.

Copy the writing below. Fill in the gaps with words from the box.

Mr Jones went to the self-service filling ______ near the Town Hall at ______ . He got out of his ______ and took off the petrol cap. Then he pressed the ______ on the side of the petrol ______ to get 3-star petrol.

He put the ______ in the tank and squeezed the trigger. He put 16 litres of petrol into the car, and it cost £ ______ altogether. He put the nozzle back in the pump. Then he went to ______ the girl for the petrol.

pay station button pump 3.60 Ashfold nozzle car

39 Working Ashfold

Twenty thousand people live in Ashfold. Some of them work there. But a lot of them work in the city, seven miles away. At one time many men worked in the coal mines and the women worked in the mills. Now one of the mines has closed down, so there is a lot of unemployment. And one or two mills have shut too, which has put some women out of work. A few school-leavers have found work in the shops in town. Some on the factory estate. But work is hard to come by. Those who have a job stick to it. For those that don't, there are only two things. One is to sign on the dole. The other is to go self-employed.

Choose a word to fill the gap. Write the word.

		Choose a Word
1	______ thousand people live in Ashfold.	five/twenty/ten
2	Many people work in the ______ .	village/city/station
3	The city is ______ miles away.	six/seventy/seven
4	The two main work places used to be coal mines and ______ .	mills/shops/miles
5	There is a lot of ______ at Ashfold.	towns/unemployment/trouble
6	Some women are unemployed because the ______ have shut down.	shops/mines/mills
7	Some school-leavers have found work on the ______ estate.	new/housing/factory
8	Some school-leavers go ______ ______ .	around town/to school/self-employed
9	Some school-leavers find work in the ______ .	shops/pubs/buses.

What work do the people in *your* family do? Are any out of work?

40 The Mill

1

2
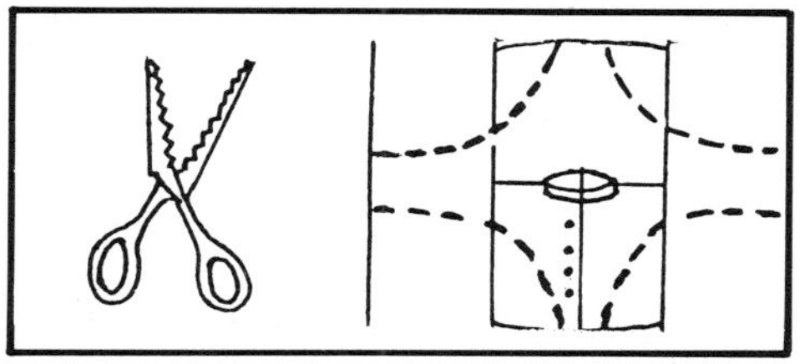

3
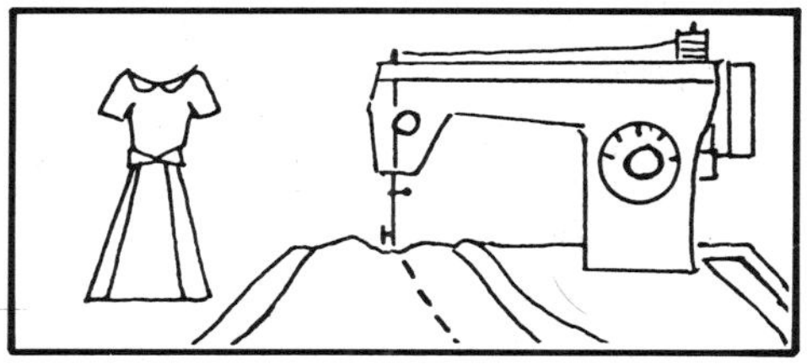

4
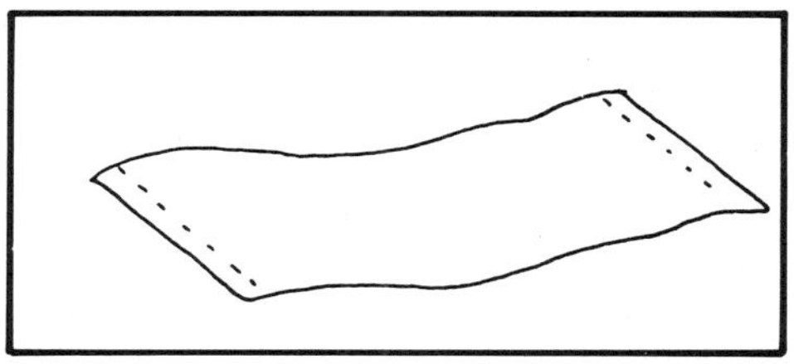

5

6

Stubbs, Wright and Walker is a mill in Ashfold. It makes clothes and sheets. The clothes are for Marks and Spencer and other places. Some of the women work at the mill part-time.

These pictures show what happens.

Match the sentence with the picture:

Clothes are bought. **6**

Clothes are sewn.

Rolls of cloth are brought to the mill.

Clothes are taken to the stores.

Cloth is marked and cut to shape.

Sheets are made.

41 Mr and Mrs Anderson

The Anderson family live near Ashfold High School – all but one. She got married last year.

Copy the chart and ring the picture-number.

1	Mrs Anderson's name is Rosa. She is 43. She is a part-time office cleaner.	2/4/7 (2 ringed)
2	Mary Anderson, 19, works in a flower shop.	2/3/4
3	Des is 16. He took his Art CSE this year.	8/2/1
4	Al is 11. He's starting at Ashfold High in September.	2/5/8
5	Gary Anderson drives a fork-lift. He's 44.	1/4/5
6	Lil Anderson's 22. She's out of work.	6/3/4
7	Dean's 20. He's a packer in his dad's firm.	7/4/6
8	Rosa married last year. She's 24, her husband is 25. She's a typist at A.G. Bamford's.	2/7/5

Al is worried about starting at Ashfold High. How did *you* feel on your first day at your new school?

42 Stubbs, Wright and Walker

This is a drawing of a big mill in Ashfold. The workers are going home at the end of the day.

1 How many cars can you see?
2 How many chimneys with smoke can you see?
3 How many windows can you see with round tops?
4 Is there a lorry in the picture?
5 Is there a crane in the picture?
6 Name the three things with two wheels you can see.
7 How many crash-helmets can you count?
8 What is the man on the push-bike wearing on his head?
9 What do you think the lorry is carrying?
10 What do you think the lady has in her bag?

There is a man with a bag behind the motorbike. Make up something about him. Begin like this: My name is . . .

43 Rolf Jones helps his father

Rolf Jones is 14. He is in his third year at Ashfold High. He has a brother named Sam, aged 7. Rolf's dad runs a newsagent's shop. His name is Alf Jones. He is 35. Rolf has no mother. She died 5 years ago. Rolf has got over it now, but he often thinks about her.

He helps in the shop on Saturdays and in the holidays. His dad pays him £1 an hour. He sells papers, magazines, comics, sweets and cigarettes. He has learnt a lot about money and can work out change very quickly. He has learnt a lot about people, too.

Copy and tick the TRUE or FALSE part.

		TRUE	FALSE
1	Rolf Jones is 35.		✓
2	Alf is Rolf's father.		
3	Rolf often thinks about his mother.		
4	Mrs Jones runs the shop.		
5	Alf earns £1 an hour.		
6	Rolf works in the shop on Saturdays.		
7	Shop work has taught Rolf a lot about money.		
8	A newsagent's sells tools.		
9	Sam is Rolf's brother.		
10	Alf Jones is 7.		

Would *you* like to work in a shop?
Why? Why not?

44 Sweets

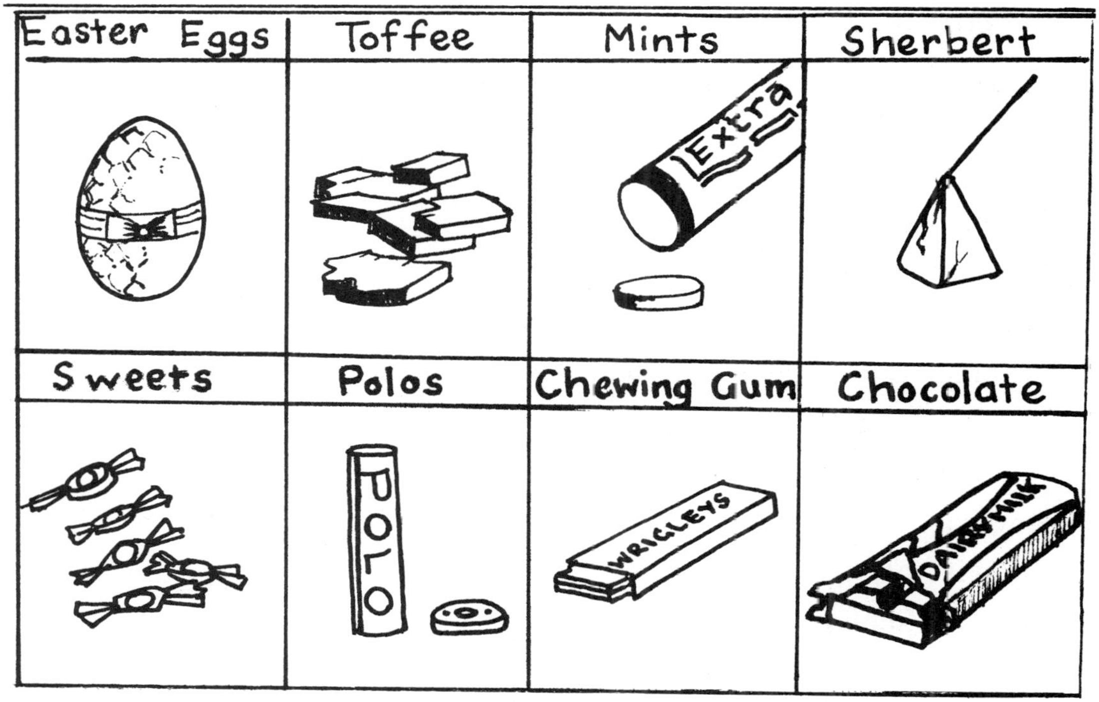

These are some of the sweets sold in Alf Jones's newsagent's shop.

Fill in the gaps with names from the pictures:

1 You buy these at Easter. __________

2 You get told off for sticking this under your desk at school. __________

3 This is a powder with a stick. __________

4 This is made from cocoa and milk and it comes in a bar. __________

5 These have a minty taste. There is a hole in the middle. __________

6 These are sold in paper wrappers. __________

7 This is made from treacle. It's sticky. __________

8 These make your mouth burn. __________

List four other kinds of sweets that you can buy from a shop.

45 Can you remember?

How much of this book do you remember?

Answer the questions and find out. Then check your answers by looking at the chapters in brackets.

1. Is there a hospital in Ashfold? (Ch 1)
2. On which street is the Town Hall? (Ch 2)
3. What is the date of Brook Farm? (Ch 3)
4. What building is next door to the clinic? (Ch 6)
5. How old is Ben Walker? (Ch 7)
6. How old is Gordon Saltman? (Ch 9)
7. How many doctors work at the Ashfold Medical Centre? (Ch 14)
8. What is Michael McLeish's mum named? (Ch 15)
9. What is Michael's grandad named? (Ch 15)
10. When is Ashfold's market day? (Ch 19)
11. Where does Mary Wong live? (Ch 20)
12. How often is Ashfold Baths open? (Ch 23)
13. Who is Dave Brown? (Ch 25)
14. When was Ashfold Football Club started? (Ch 30)
15. What kind of business does Mr White have? (Ch 33)
16. How old is Baz Wright? (Ch 36)
17. How will Michael McLeish get the money for a new bike? (Ch 38)
18. How many people live in Ashfold? (Ch 41)

Audrey Cosson remercie Emery & Cie pour leurs beaux carrelages :
www.emeryetcie.com

Direction éditoriale : Corinne Cesano
Édition : Diane Monserat
Coordination éditoriale : Candice Roger
Collaboration éditoriale : Miléna Zahalka
Direction artistique : Vu Thi
Création graphique de l'intérieur : Julia Philipps
Création et direction artistique de la couverture : Guylaine Moi
Mise en page & Photogravure : APS/Chromostyle
Fabrication : Laurence Duboscq

Solar | un département place des éditeurs

ISBN : 978-2-263-06114-1
Code éditeur : S06114
Dépôt légal : janvier 2014
Imprimé en Italie par Zanardi Group SRL

LES DÉLICES **DE SOLAR**

QUENELLES

TENDANCE

LUCIA PANTALEONI

PHOTOGRAPHIES VALÉRY GUEDES • STYLISME AUDREY COSSON

SOLAR
EDITIONS

SOMMAIRE

LA RECETTE DE BASE, PAS À PAS :

LES QUENELLES DU PRIMEUR

LES QUENELLES DU BOUCHER

LES QUENELLES DU POISSONNIER

LES QUENELLES DU PÂTISSIER

LES USTENSILES DE BASE

1. Un saladier
2. Un fouet
3. Un mixeur
4. Un grand faitout
5. Deux casseroles
6. Un plat à four
7. Deux cuillères à soupe
8. Du papier absorbant
9. Du film alimentaire
10. Une cuillère en bois
11. Une écumoire

CONSEILS POUR RÉUSSIR VOS QUENELLES

La réalisation

- Dans ce livre, vous trouverez des recettes de quenelles avec la panade traditionnelle (œuf, farine, lait), et d'autres à base de pain, de crème, de ricotta ou de pommes de terre.
- Ce n'est pas bien compliqué de faire des quenelles maison. On mixe tous les ingrédients, on façonne les quenelles, on les poche et le tour est joué !
- Le poids de chaque quenelle se situe entre 60 et 90 g.
- Les légumes tels que les poivrons ou les aubergines peuvent contenir plus ou moins d'eau. Il convient donc de les cuire au gril ou au four à chaleur tournante. Si après cette opération la pâte est encore trop molle, ajoutez 1 cuillerée à soupe de farine.

La conservation

- Toutes les quenelles dont nous vous proposons les recettes dans cet ouvrage peuvent être conservées 48 heures maximum au réfrigérateur avant d'être cuites.
- Vous pouvez congeler les quenelles. Vous les cuirez en les pochant directement dans l'eau bouillante à la sortie du congélateur. Vous compterez le temps de cuisson comme pour les quenelles non congelées, c'est-à-dire à partir de l'ébullition.

La cuisson

- Vous pouvez façonner vos quenelles avec 2 cuillères à soupe mouillées pour vous faciliter la tâche.
- Quand vous cuisinez les quenelles, ne prenez pas trop de pâte à la fois car elle gonfle à la cuisson !
- Le temps de cuisson est calculé à partir de l'ébullition.
- Pour que les quenelles ne se cassent pas, faites-les cuire dans une eau frémissante.

Le service

- Préchauffez, si possible, vos assiettes de service. Cela contribuera à maintenir le plat à la bonne température.

LA RECETTE DE BASE, PAS À PAS :
QUENELLES DE BROCHET SAUCE NANTUA

Moyenne — Moyen — Préparé à l'avance — Fête

POUR 4 PERSONNES
PRÉPARATION : 20 MIN
CUISSON : 40 MIN
RÉFRIGÉRATION : 1 H

CRÈMERIE

Œufs : 2 entiers + le blanc de 1 gros

Lait : 54 cl

Crème fleurette : 8 cl

Beurre : 120 g

Beurre d'écrevisse : 40 g

POISSONNERIE

Brochet (sandre ou perche) : 200 g (poids net)

ÉPICERIE

Farine : 120 g

Noix muscade : 2 pincées

Sel, poivre du moulin

Côtes-du-jura blanc

1 PRÉPAREZ LES INGRÉDIENTS DES QUENELLES

Mixez le brochet, avec du sel, du poivre, une pincée de noix muscade et le blanc d'œuf. Transférez dans un saladier, couvrez avec du film alimentaire et réservez au réfrigérateur. Dans une casserole, faites bouillir 14 cl de lait salé. Ajoutez du poivre et 60 g de beurre. Lorsque le beurre est fondu, retirez le récipient du feu et versez 80 g de farine en une fois. Mélangez à l'aide d'un fouet et remettez sur le feu pendant 5 minutes au minimum, sans cesser de mélanger. Quand la pâte se détache des parois, versez dans un récipient et ajoutez les 2 œufs entiers, l'un après l'autre. Laissez refroidir, puis ajoutez le brochet et mélangez. Si la pâte est trop molle, entreposez-la 1 heure au réfrigérateur.

2 FORMEZ LES QUENELLES

Prélevez 1 cuillerée à soupe de pâte (n'en prenez pas trop, car elle gonfle à la cuisson) et façonnez-la en faisant rouler la seconde cuillère autour. Passez ainsi la quenelle plusieurs fois d'une cuillère à l'autre jusqu'à ce qu'elle soit moulée. Recommencez l'opération jusqu'à épuisement de la pâte.

3 FAITES CUIRE LES QUENELLES

Dans un faitout, mettez à bouillir 4 l d'eau salée. Pochez les quenelles dans l'eau salée pendant 15 minutes. Quand elles sont cuites, égouttez-les avec une écumoire et posez-les sur du papier absorbant.

4 PRÉPAREZ LA SAUCE NANTUA

Préchauffez le four à 200 °C (th. 6-7). Dans une casserole, faites fondre 60 g de beurre, ajoutez 40 g de farine et mélangez. Laissez cuire quelques minutes puis, en vous aidant d'un fouet, incorporez 40 cl de lait. Faites cuire à feu minimum pendant 10 minutes. Incorporez la crème fleurette petit à petit. Ajoutez du sel, du poivre et une pincée de noix muscade. Faites cuire sans cesser de remuer, jusqu'à obtenir une consistance crémeuse. Éteignez le feu et incorporez le beurre d'écrevisse en fouettant. Rectifiez l'assaisonnement.

5 FAITES CUIRE L'ENSEMBLE

Dans un plat à four, déposez un peu de sauce Nantua, puis les quenelles. Couvrez avec la sauce restante et enfournez 15 minutes environ. Servez à la sortie du four.

FAIRE UN BEURRE D'ÉCREVISSE MAISON

Pour 6 personnes : 100 g de carcasses d'écrevisses, 100 g de beurre. Pilez les carcasses d'écrevisses au mortier, ajoutez le beurre pommade et pilez à nouveau jusqu'à l'obtention d'une pâte homogène. Passez au chinois. Mettez au réfrigérateur 2 heures afin que le beurre d'écrevisse durcisse.

QUENELLES AUX CÈPES

Moyenne — Moyen — Végétarien

POUR 4 PERSONNES

PRÉPARATION : 30 MIN

CUISSON : 40 MIN

CONSERVATION : 48 H
AU RÉFRIGÉRATEUR
AVANT CUISSON

CRÈMERIE

Œuf : 1 jaune

Beurre : 40 g

Parmesan fraîchement râpé : 70 g

PRIMEUR

Cèpes : 200 g frais (ou 20 g séchés)

Pommes de terre bintje, cuites à la vapeur : 800 g

Ail : 1 gousse

Persil plat : 1 bouquet

ÉPICERIE

Huile d'olive extra-vierge : 2 c. à s.

Sel, poivre du moulin

Juliénas

1 PRÉPAREZ LES INGRÉDIENTS

Épluchez et écrasez la gousse d'ail. Hachez les feuilles de persil. Faites gonfler les cèpes dans un bol d'eau bouillante salée pendant 5 minutes, puis égouttez-les et coupez-les en fines lamelles. Gardez leur eau de végétation. Préchauffez le four à 200 °C (th. 6-7).

2 CUISINEZ

Faites cuire les pommes de terre non pelées à l'autocuiseur, 20 minutes à partir du sifflement. Dans une poêle, versez l'huile et faites-y revenir l'ail. Ajoutez les cèpes (attention aux projections), une petite louche de leur eau de végétation, le persil, du sel et du poivre. Faites cuire pendant 5 minutes, en mélangeant régulièrement. Puis éteignez, ôtez la gousse d'ail et réservez la sauce. Pelez les pommes de terre cuites et passez-les au presse-purée. Mettez-les dans un saladier et mélangez-les avec le jaune d'œuf, du sel et du poivre. Incorporez la sauce aux cèpes à la purée de pommes de terre, ajoutez 15 g de beurre, 20 g de parmesan, du sel et du poivre. En vous aidant de 2 cuillères, formez les quenelles aux cèpes comme expliqué dans la recette de base p. 6 et déposez-les dans un plat allant au four.

3 FAITES CUIRE

Parsemez avec le parmesan et le beurre restants, et passez au four 20 minutes.

4 DRESSEZ

Servez bien chaud.

UNE IDÉE EN PLUS

Ces quenelles constituent l'accompagnement idéal pour un canard rôti.

QUENELLES AUX ÉPINARDS, GRATINÉES AU FOUR

Facile — Faible — Grande tablée

POUR 4 PERSONNES
PRÉPARATION : 15 MIN
CUISSON : 30 MIN
REPOS : 10 MIN
CONSERVATION : 48 H AU RÉFRIGÉRATEUR AVANT CUISSON

CRÈMERIE

Œufs : 2 jaunes
Lait entier frais : 50 cl
Beurre : 70 g
Parmesan fraîchement râpé : 50 g

PRIMEUR

Épinards frais : 170 g (ou 85 g surgelés)

ÉPICERIE

Semoule de blé fine : 100 g
Sel, poivre du moulin

Chablis

1 **PRÉPAREZ LES INGRÉDIENTS**
Lavez, essorez et émincez les épinards.

2 **CUISINEZ**
Faites bouillir le lait avec une pincée de sel et du poivre. Ajoutez la semoule en vous aidant d'un fouet, puis les épinards. Faites cuire pendant 10 minutes. Préchauffez le four à 200 °C (th. 6-7). Éloignez la préparation du feu et ajoutez les jaunes d'œufs, 20 g de beurre, du sel, du poivre et 15 g de parmesan. Versez la préparation sur une planche en bois et laissez refroidir 10 minutes. En vous aidant de 2 cuillères, formez les quenelles comme expliqué dans la recette de base p. 6 et déposez-les dans un plat allant au four préalablement beurré. Ajoutez 50 g de beurre fondu et saupoudrez avec le parmesan restant.

3 **FAITES CUIRE**
Enfournez 20 minutes environ.

4 **DRESSEZ**
Répartissez dans les assiettes et servez.

UN ACCOMPAGNEMENT IDÉAL

Vous pouvez accompagner ces quenelles de filets de daurade juste cuits à la poêle avec des tomates cerises et des petites olives taggiasche.

QUENELLES AU POTIMARRON ET AUX NOISETTES

Facile | Faible | Végétarien

POUR 4 PERSONNES
PRÉPARATION : 20 MIN
CUISSON : 42 MIN
REPOS : 10 MIN
CONSERVATION : 48 H AU RÉFRIGÉRATEUR AVANT CUISSON

CRÈMERIE

Œufs : 2
Lait : 12 cl
Crème fleurette : 7 cl
Ricotta : 250 g
Parmesan fraîchement râpé : 110 g

PRIMEUR

Potimarron : 250 g

ÉPICERIE

Farine : 150 g
Noix muscade : 1 pincée
Noisettes grillées : 100 g
Sel, poivre du moulin

Pinot gris d'Alsace

1 PRÉPAREZ LES INGRÉDIENTS

Découpez le potimarron en fines tranches. Concassez les noisettes. Préchauffez le four à 200 °C (th. 6-7).

2 CUISINEZ

Déposez les tranches de potimarron sur la plaque du four recouverte de papier sulfurisé et faites-les cuire 30 minutes. Puis mixez-les et laissez-les refroidir 10 minutes. Dans un saladier, mélangez la ricotta, le potimarron mixé, les œufs, la farine, la noix muscade, 30 g de parmesan, du sel et du poivre. En vous aidant de 2 cuillères, formez les quenelles comme expliqué dans la recette de base p. 6.

3 FAITES CUIRE

Faites pocher les quenelles dans 4 litres d'eau bouillante salée. Dès la reprise de l'ébullition, baissez le feu pour ne maintenir qu'un léger frémissement. Laissez cuire pendant 12 minutes. Puis égouttez-les avec une écumoire et posez-les quelques instants sur du papier absorbant. Pendant ce temps, dans une poêle faites chauffer ensemble le lait et la crème. Incorporez le parmesan restant en vous aidant d'un fouet et faites réduire pour obtenir une sauce onctueuse.

4 DRESSEZ

Répartissez les quenelles dans les assiettes, arrosez-les de crème et parsemez de noisettes concassées.

POUR UNE VERSION RÉSERVÉE AUX ADULTES

Vous pouvez remplacer les noisettes par 8 biscuits amaretti émiettés.

QUENELLES AU BASILIC, SAUCE AUX POIVRONS

Moyenne   Faible   Végétarien

POUR 4 PERSONNES
PRÉPARATION : 10 MIN
CUISSON : 30 MIN
CONSERVATION : 48 H AU RÉFRIGÉRATEUR AVANT CUISSON

CRÈMERIE

Œufs : 2 moyens
Lait : 17 cl
Beurre : 70 g
Parmesan râpé : 2 c. à s.

PRIMEUR

Basilic : 30 g de feuilles + ½ botte
Ail : 1 gousse
Oignon : 1
Poivron rouge : 1 moyen
Piment sec : 1

ÉPICERIE

Farine : 100 g
Pulpe de tomate : 1 boîte
Huile d'olive : 3 c. à s.
Sel, poivre du moulin

Chardonnay

1 PRÉPAREZ LES INGRÉDIENTS

Lavez le poivron et coupez-le en dés de 2 cm environ. Hachez les 30 g de feuilles de basilic et coupez les feuilles de la botte à la main. Pelez et émincez l'oignon et l'ail.

2 CUISINEZ

Remplissez un faitout d'eau et mettez-la à bouillir. Dans une autre casserole, faites bouillir le lait avec du sel, du poivre et le beurre. Hors du feu, versez la farine en une fois, mélangez à l'aide d'un fouet et remettez sur le feu 5 minutes, sans cesser de mélanger. Quand la pâte se détache des parois, versez-la dans un saladier, ajoutez le basilic haché, le parmesan et les œufs l'un après l'autre. En vous aidant de 2 cuillères, formez les quenelles comme expliqué dans la recette de base p. 6.

3 FAITES CUIRE

Faites pocher les quenelles dans 4 litres d'eau bouillante salée. Dès la reprise de l'ébullition, baissez le feu pour ne maintenir qu'un léger frémissement. Laissez cuire 15 minutes. Pendant ce temps, faites revenir l'ail et l'oignon dans l'huile. Émiettez le piment par-dessus, ajoutez la pulpe de tomate, les dés de poivron, du sel et laissez cuire 15 minutes environ. Ajoutez le basilic coupé à la main, 5 minutes environ avant la fin de la cuisson.

4 DRESSEZ

Égouttez les quenelles au basilic et servez-les en portions accompagnées de leur sauce aux poivrons.

DU POIVRON À L'AUBERGINE...

Certaines personnes digèrent mal le poivron ; vous pouvez lui substituer 2 petites aubergines, que vous couperez en dés de la même façon.

QUENELLES À LA BROUSSE ET À LA MENTHE, CRÈME D'ARTICHAUTS

Facile — Faible — Préparé à l'avance — Végétarien

POUR 4 PERSONNES
PRÉPARATION : 15 MIN
CUISSON : 15 MIN
CONSERVATION : 48 H AU RÉFRIGÉRATEUR AVANT CUISSON

CRÈMERIE

Œufs : 2 jaunes
Crème fleurette : 2 c. à s.
Brousse ou chèvre frais : 500 g

PRIMEUR

Menthe : 10 grandes feuilles
Persil plat : 1 botte
Fonds d'artichauts : 650 g
Ail : 1 gousse

ÉPICERIE

Farine : 70 g
Fécule de pomme de terre : 30 g
Bouillon chaud : 60 cl
Huile d'olive extra-vierge : 2 c. à s.
Sel, poivre du moulin

1 PRÉPAREZ LES INGRÉDIENTS

Pelez la gousse d'ail. Lavez et hachez les feuilles de menthe et de persil. Coupez les fonds d'artichauts en morceaux.

2 CUISINEZ

Dans un saladier, travaillez ensemble, avec une cuillère en bois, la brousse, la farine, la fécule, la menthe, les jaunes d'œufs, du sel et du poivre. En vous aidant de 2 cuillères, formez les quenelles comme expliqué dans la recette de base p. 6.

3 FAITES CUIRE

Faites pocher les quenelles dans 4 litres d'eau bouillante salée. Dès la reprise de l'ébullition, baissez le feu pour ne maintenir qu'un léger frémissement. Laissez cuire 12 minutes. Dans un autocuiseur, faites revenir l'ail dans l'huile. Ajoutez les fonds d'artichauts, le persil et laissez cuire 2 minutes. Ajoutez le bouillon, fermez l'autocuiseur et comptez 8 minutes à partir du sifflement.

4 DRESSEZ

Mixez les artichauts avec la crème fleurette. Salez, poivrez et transférez dans les assiettes de service. Égouttez les quenelles avec une écumoire, mettez-les quelques instants sur du papier absorbant et déposez-les sur la crème d'artichauts. Servez sans tarder.

LE PETIT PLUS D'UN DRESSAGE PARFAIT

Vous pouvez poser sur la crème d'artichauts 2 crevettes roses par portion, pour ajouter une touche de couleur.

QUENELLES RICOTTA ET ÉPINARDS

Facile · Faible · Grande tablée

POUR 4 PERSONNES
PRÉPARATION : 10 MIN
CUISSON : 20 MIN
REPOS : 10 MIN
CONSERVATION : 48 H AU RÉFRIGÉRATEUR AVANT CUISSON

CRÈMERIE

Œuf : 1 jaune
Crème fleurette : 25 cl
Ricotta : 500 g
Parmesan fraîchement râpé : 2 c. à s.
Vacherin : 200 g

PRIMEUR

Épinards : 300 g (ou 150 g surgelés)

ÉPICERIE

Farine : 120 g
Noix muscade : 1 pincée
Sel, poivre du moulin

Apremont

1 PRÉPAREZ LES INGRÉDIENTS

Ôtez la croûte du vacherin et coupez-le en dés.

2 CUISINEZ

Faites cuire les épinards dans une casserole d'eau bouillante salée pendant 5 minutes. Puis égouttez-les très soigneusement, laissez-les refroidir 10 minutes et coupez-les au couteau. Dans un saladier, mélangez la ricotta, la farine, la noix muscade, du sel, du poivre, le parmesan, le jaune d'œuf et les épinards. En vous aidant de 2 cuillères, formez les quenelles comme expliqué dans la recette de base p. 6.

3 FAITES CUIRE

Faites pocher les quenelles dans 4 litres d'eau bouillante salée. Dès la reprise de l'ébullition, baissez le feu pour ne maintenir qu'un léger frémissement. Laissez cuire 15 minutes. Pendant ce temps, dans une casserole, faites fondre à feu doux le vacherin et la crème. Ajoutez du poivre.

4 DRESSEZ

Égouttez les quenelles avec une écumoire, posez-les quelques instants sur du papier absorbant, puis sur les assiettes. Nappez-les avec la crème au vacherin et servez.

POUR UNE VARIANTE AUX ORTIES OU AU GORGONZOLA

Pour une touche originale, remplacez les épinards par la même quantité d'orties : recueillez ces dernières avec des gants, lavez-les et procédez comme pour les épinards, mais toujours avec des gants. Après les avoir ébouillantées, vous pourrez les manipuler à mains nues. Pour un plat au goût plus prononcé, faites fondre 200 g de gorgonzola avec 2 cuillerées à soupe de crème fleurette. Dans une autre casserole, antiadhésive et sans ajout de matière grasse, faites rissoler 100 g de lardons ; nappez les quenelles de cette crème au gorgonzola et parsemez-les de lardons.

QUENELLES À LA CRÈME ONCTUEUSE DE PARMESAN

Facile — Faible — Grande tablée

POUR 4 PERSONNES
PRÉPARATION : 15 MIN
CUISSON : 20 MIN
CONSERVATION : 48 H AU RÉFRIGÉRATEUR AVANT CUISSON

CRÈMERIE

Œufs : 2 + 1 jaune
Lait : 17 cl
Crème fleurette : 25 cl
Beurre : 70 g
Parmesan fraîchement râpé : 125 g

ÉPICERIE

Farine : 100 g
Noix muscade : 1 pincée
Sel, poivre du moulin

Morgon

1 CUISINEZ

Dans une casserole, faites bouillir le lait avec du sel, la muscade et du poivre, puis ajoutez le beurre. Lorsque le beurre est fondu, retirez le récipient du feu et versez la farine en une fois. Mélangez à l'aide d'un fouet et remettez sur le feu 5 minutes, sans cesser de mélanger. Quand la pâte se détache des parois, versez dans un récipient, ajoutez les œufs l'un après l'autre et 30 g de parmesan. En vous aidant de 2 cuillères, formez les quenelles comme expliqué dans la recette de base p. 6.

2 FAITES CUIRE

Faites pocher les quenelles dans 4 litres d'eau bouillante salée. Dès la reprise de l'ébullition, baissez le feu pour ne maintenir qu'un léger frémissement. Laissez cuire 12 minutes. Quelques minutes avant la fin de la cuisson, portez la crème fleurette à ébullition dans une casserole, puis versez le parmesan restant et mélangez avec un fouet. Enlevez le récipient du feu, ajoutez le jaune d'œuf et continuez à fouetter.

3 DRESSEZ

Égouttez les quenelles avec une écumoire, posez-les quelques instants sur du papier absorbant, puis sur les assiettes. Arrosez avec la crème de parmesan et servez aussitôt.

LE GOÛT EN PLUS

Pour le parmesan, choisissez un beau morceau affiné 24 mois en moyenne.

QUENELLES AUX POIVRONS ROUGES, SAUCE AUX HERBES AROMATIQUES

Facile — Faible — Grande tablée

POUR 4 PERSONNES
PRÉPARATION : 10 MIN
CUISSON : 35 MIN
CONSERVATION : 48 H AU RÉFRIGÉRATEUR AVANT CUISSON

CRÈMERIE
Œuf : 1 jaune
Crème fleurette : 20 cl
Beurre : 20 g

PRIMEUR
Pommes de terre : 500 g
Poivrons rouges : 200 g
Ail : 1 gousse
Échalote : 1
Basilic : ½ bouquet
Romarin : les feuilles de 2 tiges

ÉPICERIE
Farine : 120 g
Origan : 2 belles pincées
Sel, poivre du moulin

Rosé de Provence

1 **PRÉPAREZ LES INGRÉDIENTS**
Hachez les poivrons et faites-les égoutter soigneusement dans une passoire. Hachez les feuilles de romarin et le basilic. Pelez et hachez l'ail et l'échalote.

2 **CUISINEZ**
Faites cuire les pommes de terre dans l'autocuiseur pendant 20 minutes à partir du sifflement. Passez-les au presse-purée, puis mélangez-les avec les poivrons, la farine, le jaune d'œuf, du sel et du poivre. En vous aidant de 2 cuillères, formez les quenelles comme expliqué dans la recette de base p. 6.

3 **FAITES CUIRE**
Faites pocher les quenelles dans 4 litres d'eau bouillante salée. Dès la reprise de l'ébullition, baissez le feu pour ne maintenir qu'un léger frémissement. Laissez cuire 15 minutes. Pendant ce temps, préparez la sauce : faites revenir pendant quelques instants le romarin, le basilic, l'origan, l'ail et l'échalote dans le beurre, puis ajoutez la crème, du sel et du poivre.

4 **DRESSEZ**
Servez sans tarder les quenelles nappées de sauce aux herbes.

POUR UN MENU IDÉAL
Vous pouvez faire suivre ces quenelles d'une pintade rôtie accompagnée d'aubergines et de poivrons.

QUENELLES AUX ASPERGES, CRÈME DE BREBIS AFFINÉ

Moyenne — Faible — Végétarien

POUR 4 PERSONNES
PRÉPARATION : 15 MIN
CUISSON : 22 MIN
CONSERVATION : 48 H AU RÉFRIGÉRATEUR AVANT CUISSON

CRÈMERIE

Œuf : 1 jaune
Lait : 15 cl
Fromage de brebis affiné ou parmesan râpé : 150 g
Parmesan : 2 c. à s.
Ricotta : 80 g

PRIMEUR

Asperges vertes : 350 g
Persil plat : ½ botte
Ail : 1 gousse

ÉPICERIE

Farine : 80 g
Huile d'olive : 2 c. à s.
Sel, poivre du moulin

Meursault

1 PRÉPAREZ LES INGRÉDIENTS

Enlevez la partie fibreuse des asperges et coupez-les en rondelles. Lavez et hachez les feuilles de persil. Pelez la gousse d'ail. Égouttez soigneusement la ricotta.

2 CUISINEZ

Dans une poêle, versez l'huile et faites-y revenir l'ail. Ajoutez les asperges, le persil, du poivre, du sel et 1 cm d'eau. Faites cuire à couvert pendant 10 minutes. Au bout de ce temps, ôtez l'ail et passez les asperges au mixeur. Dans un saladier, mettez les asperges mixées, la farine, le jaune d'œuf, le parmesan, la ricotta, du poivre et du sel. Si nécessaire, ajoutez 1 cuillerée à soupe de farine. En vous aidant de 2 cuillères, formez les quenelles comme expliqué dans la recette de base p. 6.

3 FAITES CUIRE

Faites pocher les quenelles dans 4 litres d'eau bouillante salée. Dès la reprise de l'ébullition, baissez le feu pour ne maintenir qu'un léger frémissement. Laissez cuire 12 minutes. Entre-temps, faites fondre le fromage de brebis dans le lait jusqu'à l'obtention d'une crème.

4 DRESSEZ

Disposez de la crème de fromage dans le fond de 4 assiettes creuses préchauffées. Égouttez les quenelles avec une écumoire et posez-les quelques instants sur du papier absorbant. Répartissez-les dans les assiettes et nappez-les avec le reste de crème de fromage de brebis. Donnez quelques tours de moulin à poivre et servez sans tarder.

POUR UN MENU IDÉAL

Vous pouvez faire suivre ces quenelles d'une daurade cuite au four avec des tomates cerises, des olives noires et du thym.

QUENELLES AUX AUBERGINES ET À LA MENTHE

Facile | Faible | Préparé à l'avance | Grande tablée

POUR 4 PERSONNES
PRÉPARATION : 20 MIN
CUISSON : 40 MIN
REPOS : 30 MIN
CONSERVATION : 48 H AU RÉFRIGÉRATEUR AVANT CUISSON

CRÈMERIE

Œuf : 1 jaune
Parmesan : 3 c. à s.

PRIMEUR

Aubergines fraîches : 800 g
Pommes de terre : 300 g
Menthe : 30 feuilles
Ail : 1 gousse
Piment sec : 1 petit

ÉPICERIE

Farine : 215 g
Pulpe de tomate : 1 boîte
Huile d'olive extra-vierge : 2 c. à s.
Sel, poivre du moulin

Vouvray sec

1 PRÉPAREZ LES INGRÉDIENTS

Lavez les feuilles de menthe. Dégermez la gousse d'ail. Coupez les aubergines en deux et incisez la pulpe en croisillons.

2 CUISINEZ

Passez les aubergines au four à micro-ondes pendant 5 minutes à la puissance maximum, puis au gril 10 minutes. Laissez-les tiédir 30 minutes. Faites cuire les pommes de terre dans l'autocuiseur pendant 20 minutes à partir du sifflement. Pendant ce temps, faites revenir l'ail avec l'huile. Émiettez le piment par-dessus, ajoutez la pulpe de tomate, du sel et du poivre. Laissez cuire 15 minutes environ, puis gardez au chaud. Récupérez la pulpe des aubergines et mixez-la avec les feuilles de menthe. Dans un saladier, passez les pommes de terre au presse-purée. Ajoutez-leur la farine, le parmesan, le jaune d'œuf, les aubergines à la menthe, du poivre et du sel. En vous aidant de 2 cuillères, formez les quenelles comme expliqué dans la recette de base p. 6.

3 FAITES CUIRE

Faites pocher les quenelles dans 4 litres d'eau bouillante salée. Dès la reprise de l'ébullition, baissez le feu pour ne maintenir qu'un léger frémissement. Laissez cuire 12 minutes.

4 DRESSEZ

Égouttez les quenelles avec une écumoire, posez-les quelques instants sur du papier absorbant puis sur les assiettes. Nappez de sauce tomate et servez sans tarder.

POUR UN MENU IDÉAL

Vous pouvez faire suivre ces quenelles d'une poêlée de fruits de mer : faites sauter ces derniers avec juste un peu d'huile, de l'ail et du persil.

QUENELLES À LA RICOTTA ET AUX ZESTES DE MANDARINES

Moyenne — Faible — Végétarien

POUR 4 PERSONNES
PRÉPARATION : 15 MIN
CUISSON : 15 MIN
CONSERVATION : 48 H AU RÉFRIGÉRATEUR AVANT CUISSON

CRÈMERIE

Œufs : 2 jaunes
Crème fleurette : 20 cl
Beurre : 30 g
Ricotta : 700 g
Parmesan : 30 g

PRIMEUR

Mandarines : le zeste de 4
Échalotes : 2
Thym : 2 branches

ÉPICERIE

Farine : 80 g
Fécule de pomme de terre : 50 g
Vin blanc sec : 40 cl
Sel, poivre du moulin

Sauvignon blanc

1 PRÉPAREZ LES INGRÉDIENTS

Pelez les échalotes et coupez-les en deux.

2 CUISINEZ

Dans un saladier, mélangez la ricotta, les zestes de mandarines, les œufs, la farine, la fécule de pomme de terre, le parmesan, du sel et du poivre. En vous aidant de 2 cuillères, formez les quenelles comme expliqué dans la recette de base p. 6.

3 FAITES CUIRE

Faites pocher les quenelles dans 4 litres d'eau bouillante salée. Dès la reprise de l'ébullition, baissez le feu pour ne maintenir qu'un léger frémissement. Laissez cuire 15 minutes. Pendant ce temps, versez le vin dans une casserole avec les échalotes et le thym. Faites réduire de moitié, puis réservez au chaud. Dans une poêle, versez la crème fleurette, ajoutez le vin réduit et filtré, mélangez et faites bouillir quelques minutes, jusqu'à l'obtention d'une sauce sirupeuse. Ajoutez alors le beurre, du sel, du poivre et mélangez.

4 DRESSEZ

Égouttez les quenelles avec une écumoire, posez-les quelques instants sur du papier absorbant, puis servez-les avec leur sauce.

LA QUALITÉ DES PRODUITS

Privilégiez la ricotta d'un bon fromager, elle n'en sera que meilleure.

QUENELLES AU PERSIL ET AUX PETITS POIS

Moyenne — Faible — Fête

POUR 4 PERSONNES
PRÉPARATION : 30 MIN
CUISSON : 40 MIN
CONSERVATION : 48 H AU RÉFRIGÉRATEUR AVANT CUISSON

CRÈMERIE

Œufs : 2
Lait : 34 cl
Beurre : 170 g

CHARCUTERIE

Jambon blanc : 70 g

PRIMEUR

Petits pois extra-fins : 170 g (poids net)
Persil plat : 1 bouquet

ÉPICERIE

Farine : 150 g
Noix muscade : 1 pincée
Sel, poivre du moulin

Chinon

1 PRÉPAREZ LES INGRÉDIENTS

Lavez et hachez les feuilles de persil. Coupez le jambon en fines lamelles.

2 CUISINEZ

Faites cuire les petits pois 20 minutes dans de l'eau bouillante salée. Pour la béchamel, dans une casserole, faites fondre 100 g de beurre, ajoutez 30 g de farine et mélangez. Laissez cuire jusqu'à légère coloration. Ajoutez le lait, portez à léger frémissement et laissez mijoter encore 15 minutes à feu très doux, en remuant constamment. Puis éteignez le feu, salez, poivrez et ajoutez la muscade. Incorporez enfin les petits pois, le jambon coupé en lamelles et réservez. Dans une autre casserole, pour les quenelles, faites bouillir 170 cl d'eau salée avec 70 g de beurre. Lorsque le beurre est fondu, retirez le récipient du feu et versez 120 g de farine et le persil. Mélangez à l'aide d'un fouet et remettez sur le feu pendant 5 minutes, sans cesser de remuer. Quand la pâte se détache des parois, versez dans un saladier. Ajoutez les œufs et mélangez. En vous aidant de 2 cuillères, formez les quenelles comme expliqué dans la recette de base p. 6.

3 FAITES CUIRE

Faites pocher les quenelles dans 4 litres d'eau bouillante salée. Dès la reprise de l'ébullition, baissez le feu pour ne maintenir qu'un léger frémissement. Laissez cuire 15 minutes.

4 DRESSEZ

Égouttez les quenelles, posez-les quelques instants sur du papier absorbant et servez-les avec la béchamel aux petits pois et au jambon.

POUR UNE VERSION GRATINÉE

Vous pouvez également gratiner les quenelles : saupoudrez-les de 70 g de parmesan et passez-les 20 minutes au four préchauffé à 180 °C (th. 6). Dans ce cas, la cuisson à l'eau sera de 5 minutes seulement.

QUENELLES DE LAPIN À LA MOUTARDE

Facile — Faible — Tradition

POUR 4 PERSONNES
PRÉPARATION : 10 MIN
CUISSON : 20 MIN
CONSERVATION : 48 H AU RÉFRIGÉRATEUR AVANT CUISSON

CRÈMERIE

Crème fleurette : 15 cl
Œuf : 1 blanc

BOUCHERIE

Râble de lapin désossé : 600 g

PRIMEUR

Citron : le jus de ½
Échalotes : 2
Sauge : 3 grandes feuilles

ÉPICERIE

Moutarde à l'ancienne : 3 c. à c.
Vin blanc sec : 50 cl
Sel, poivre du moulin

Épineuil rouge

1 PRÉPAREZ LES INGRÉDIENTS

Pelez et hachez les échalotes.

2 CUISINEZ

Hachez au mixeur le lapin avec la crème, le blanc d'œuf, du sel et du poivre. Préchauffez le four à 180 °C (th. 6). En vous aidant de 2 cuillères, formez les quenelles comme expliqué dans la recette de base p. 6 et transférez-les sur la plaque à four doublée de papier sulfurisé ; ajoutez le vin blanc et les échalotes.

3 FAITES CUIRE

Faites cuire pendant 15 minutes, puis récupérez le jus et gardez les quenelles au chaud. Dans une casserole, faites réduire la sauce de moitié, ajoutez la moutarde, le jus de citron, les feuilles de sauge et laissez bouillir pendant 2 minutes.

4 DRESSEZ

Servez sans tarder les quenelles nappées de sauce à la moutarde.

POUR UNE VERSION AU POULET

Vous pouvez remplacer le lapin par la même quantité de blanc de poulet.

QUENELLES AU FOIE DE VEAU ET À LA SAUGE

Moyenne — Élevé — Fête

POUR 4 PERSONNES
PRÉPARATION : 25 MIN
TREMPAGE : 10 MIN
CUISSON : 22 MIN
CONSERVATION : 48 H AU RÉFRIGÉRATEUR AVANT CUISSON

CRÈMERIE

Œufs : 2
Lait : ½ bol
Beurre : 80 g
Parmesan : 2 c. à s.

BOUCHERIE

Foie de veau : 150 g
Lard fumé : 80 g

PRIMEUR

Échalote : 1
Ail : 1 gousse
Persil plat : 1 petite botte
Sauge : 4 grandes feuilles

ÉPICERIE

Mie de pain : 60 g
Noix muscade : 1 bonne pincée
Semoule fine : 3 c. à s.
Sel, poivre du moulin

1 PRÉPAREZ LES INGRÉDIENTS

Épluchez et hachez l'échalote. Épluchez et dégermez l'ail. Lavez les feuilles de persil. Versez le lait dans un bol et mettez-y la mie de pain à tremper 10 minutes environ. Puis essorez-la soigneusement. Dans un autre bol, mettez les œufs et battez-les à la fourchette. Coupez le lard fumé en dés.

2 CUISINEZ

Faites revenir l'échalote et l'ail dans 20 g de beurre pendant 2 minutes. Ajoutez le lard fumé et continuez la cuisson 3 minutes supplémentaires. Ajoutez le foie de veau, le persil, du poivre, du sel et continuez la cuisson encore 5 minutes. Passez la mie de pain au mixeur avec le mélange au foie de veau. Transférez l'appareil dans un saladier, ajoutez le parmesan, la semoule, la muscade et les œufs battus. Mélangez soigneusement et rectifiez l'assaisonnement. En vous aidant de 2 cuillères, formez les quenelles comme expliqué dans la recette de base p. 6.

3 FAITES CUIRE

Faites pocher les quenelles dans 4 litres d'eau bouillante salée. Dès la reprise de l'ébullition, baissez le feu pour ne maintenir qu'un léger frémissement. Laissez cuire 12 minutes.

4 DRESSEZ

Faites fondre le beurre restant avec la sauge. Égouttez les quenelles avec une écumoire, puis faites-les sauter quelques instants dans le beurre à la sauge et servez-les en portions.

LE CONSEIL

Pour éviter que le beurre ne brûle à la cuisson, ajoutez 1 cuillerée à café d'huile d'olive.

QUENELLES À LA MOELLE ET LEUR BOUILLON

Facile | Faible | Grande tablée

POUR 4 PERSONNES
PRÉPARATION : 5 MIN
CUISSON : 5 MIN
CONSERVATION : 48 H AU RÉFRIGÉRATEUR AVANT CUISSON

CRÈMERIE

Œufs : 2

BOUCHERIE

Moelle de bœuf : 200 g

PRIMEUR

Ail : 1 gousse
Oignon blanc : 1
Persil plat : ½ botte

ÉPICERIE

Farine : 40 g
Chapelure : 90 g
Noix muscade : 1 pincée
Bouillon de bœuf : 1 l
Sel, poivre du moulin

Vacqueyras

1 PRÉPAREZ LES INGRÉDIENTS

Pelez l'oignon blanc et coupez-le en morceaux. Épluchez et dégermez l'ail. Lavez les feuilles de persil. Faites chauffer le bouillon de bœuf.

2 CUISINEZ

Hachez la moelle de bœuf avec le persil, la farine, la chapelure, l'oignon, l'ail, les œufs, du sel, du poivre et la muscade. Mélangez soigneusement. En vous aidant de 2 cuillères, formez les quenelles comme expliqué dans la recette de base p. 6.

3 FAITES CUIRE

Faites pocher les quenelles dans 4 litres d'eau bouillante salée. Dès la reprise de l'ébullition, baissez le feu pour ne maintenir qu'un léger frémissement. Laissez cuire 5 minutes.

4 DRESSEZ

Répartissez les quenelles dans des assiettes creuses et servez-les avec leur bouillon.

UNE CHAPELURE MAISON

Vous obtiendrez une excellente chapelure maison en faisant griller du vieux pain et en le mixant.

QUENELLES DE VOLAILLE AUX MORILLES ET LEUR BOUILLON

Facile — Moyen — Fête

POUR 4 PERSONNES
PRÉPARATION : 15 MIN
TREMPAGE : 15 MIN
CUISSON : 12 MIN
CONSERVATION : 48 H AU RÉFRIGÉRATEUR AVANT CUISSON

CRÈMERIE
Œuf : 3 blancs
Crème fleurette : 22 cl
Beurre : 30 g

BOUCHERIE-CHARCUTERIE
Blanc de volaille : 220 g

PRIMEUR
Échalote : 1

ÉPICERIE
Morilles séchées : 30 g
Bouillon de volaille : 60 cl
Sel, poivre du moulin

Puligny-montrachet

1 **PRÉPAREZ LES INGRÉDIENTS**
Pelez et hachez l'échalote. Plongez les morilles dans un bol d'eau chaude pendant 15 minutes.

2 **CUISINEZ**
Dans une poêle, mettez le beurre et faites revenir très doucement les morilles avec l'échalote. Réservez. Passez le blanc de volaille au mixeur avec les blancs d'œufs que vous ajouterez l'un après l'autre, la crème, la sauce aux morilles, du sel et du poivre. En vous aidant de 2 cuillères, formez les quenelles comme expliqué dans la recette de base p. 6.

3 **FAITES CUIRE**
Faites pocher les quenelles dans le bouillon de volaille. Dès la reprise de l'ébullition, baissez le feu pour ne maintenir qu'un léger frémissement. Laissez cuire 8 minutes.

4 **DRESSEZ**
Servez les quenelles avec leur bouillon.

POUR UN DRESSAGE PARFAIT
Pour ajouter une touche de couleur, vous pouvez décorer ce plat avec quelques pointes d'asperges vertes : mettez-les dans une casserole d'eau froide, faites-les cuire 5 minutes et épongez-les aussitôt.

QUENELLES DE SAINT-JACQUES

Facile — Moyen — Fête

POUR 4 PERSONNES

PRÉPARATION : 10 MIN

CONSERVATION : 48 H
AU RÉFRIGÉRATEUR
AVANT CUISSON

CUISSON : 20 MIN

CRÈMERIE

Œuf : 1 blanc

Crème fleurette : 60 cl

Beurre : 30 g

PRIMEUR

Champignons de Paris : 400 g

Échalote : 1

Persil plat : ½ botte

POISSONNERIE

Noix de saint-jacques : 320 g

ÉPICERIE

Huile d'olive extra-vierge : 1 c. à s.

Sel, poivre du moulin

Sancerre blanc

1 PRÉPAREZ LES INGRÉDIENTS

Pelez et émincez l'échalote. Lavez et hachez les feuilles du persil plat. Coupez les pieds des champignons, lavez-les rapidement à l'eau claire, essuyez-les et coupez-les en petits morceaux.

2 CUISINEZ

Mixez les noix de saint-jacques avec 40 cl de crème et le blanc d'œuf. Salez, poivrez et entreposez au réfrigérateur. Dans une poêle, faites revenir l'échalote dans l'huile et le beurre. Ajoutez les champignons, le persil, du sel, du poivre et faites cuire à feu vif pendant 10 minutes. Ajoutez 20 cl de crème et faites réduire à feu vif pendant 5 minutes. Mixez, rectifiez l'assaisonnement. Réservez au chaud. Sortez la préparation du réfrigérateur et, en vous aidant de 2 cuillères, formez les quenelles comme expliqué dans la recette de base p. 6.

3 FAITES CUIRE

Faites pocher les quenelles dans 4 litres d'eau bouillante salée. Dès la reprise de l'ébullition, baissez le feu pour ne maintenir qu'un léger frémissement. Laissez cuire 4 minutes.

4 DRESSEZ

Nappez les quenelles avec la sauce chaude. Donnez quelques tours de moulin à poivre et servez aussitôt.

POUR UNE VERSION FESTIVE

Pour un plat encore plus festif, vous pouvez remplacer les champignons de Paris par des cèpes.

QUENELLES AU LIEU JAUNE, SAUCE AU CURRY

Facile — Faible — Cuisine du monde

POUR 4 PERSONNES
PRÉPARATION : 10 MIN
CUISSON : 23 MIN
CONSERVATION : 48 H AU RÉFRIGÉRATEUR AVANT CUISSON

CRÈMERIE

Œufs : 2 jaunes + 1 blanc
Lait frais : 4 cl
Crème fleurette : 27,5 cl
Beurre : 10 g

POISSONNERIE

Lieu jaune : 500 g (poids net)

ÉPICERIE

Farine : 15 g
Curry : ½ c. à s.
Sel, poivre du moulin

Pouilly-fuissé

1 CUISINEZ

Dans une casserole, faites fondre le beurre, ajoutez la farine et mélangez pour l'incorporer. Faites cuire jusqu'à légère coloration (roux). Ajoutez le lait graduellement, puis 12,5 cl de crème. Portez à léger frémissement et laissez mijoter encore 10 minutes à feu très doux, en remuant constamment. Salez, poivrez et ajoutez le curry. Hors du feu, incorporez les jaunes d'œufs en fouettant. Réservez au chaud. Hachez le lieu jaune au mixeur avec 15 cl de crème, le blanc d'œuf, du sel et du poivre. En vous aidant de 2 cuillères, formez les quenelles comme expliqué dans la recette de base p. 6.

2 FAITES CUIRE

Faites pocher les quenelles dans 4 litres d'eau bouillante salée. Dès la reprise de l'ébullition, baissez le feu pour ne maintenir qu'un léger frémissement. Laissez cuire 8 minutes.

3 DRESSEZ

Égouttez les quenelles avec une écumoire, posez-les quelques instants sur du papier absorbant, puis sur les assiettes. Nappez avec la béchamel au curry et servez.

UN ACCOMPAGNEMENT IDÉAL

Vous pouvez accompagner ces quenelles de morceaux de poulet sautés dans un peu d'huile avec de l'ail et du curcuma.

QUENELLES DE CABILLAUD, CRÈME DE POMMES DE TERRE ET PERSIL

Facile — Faible — Végétarien

POUR 4 PERSONNES

PRÉPARATION : 10 MIN

CUISSON : 20 MIN

CONSERVATION : 48 H AU RÉFRIGÉRATEUR AVANT CUISSON

CRÈMERIE

Œuf : 1 blanc

Crème fleurette : 20 cl

POISSONNERIE

Dos de cabillaud sans arêtes ni peau : 600 g

PRIMEUR

Oignon : 1

Persil plat : 2 belles bottes

Ail : 1 gousse dégermée

ÉPICERIE

Bouillon de légumes : 80 cl

Pommes de terre : 3 moyennes

Huile d'olive extra-vierge : 2 c. à s.

Sel, poivre du moulin

Bourgogne-aligoté

1 PRÉPAREZ LES INGRÉDIENTS

Pelez, épluchez et émincez l'oignon. Épluchez et dégermez l'ail. Lavez les feuilles de persil. Pelez les pommes de terre et coupez-les en cubes.

2 CUISINEZ

Passez le cabillaud au mixeur avec la crème, la gousse d'ail, le blanc d'œuf, quelques feuilles de persil, du sel et du poivre. Réservez au frais. En vous aidant de 2 cuillères, formez les quenelles comme expliqué dans la recette de base p. 6.

3 FAITES CUIRE

Dans un autocuiseur, faites revenir l'oignon dans l'huile avec les pommes de terre pendant 10 minutes. Ajoutez les feuilles de persil (gardez-en quelques-unes pour la décoration), le bouillon de légumes, du poivre, du sel. Fermez l'autocuiseur et faites cuire 10 minutes à partir du sifflement. Puis retirez du feu, mixez et gardez au chaud. Faites pocher les quenelles dans 4 litres d'eau bouillante salée. Dès la reprise de l'ébullition, baissez le feu pour ne maintenir qu'un léger frémissement. Laissez cuire 2 à 3 minutes.

4 DRESSEZ

Dressez la sauce dans 4 assiettes creuses préchauffées. Égouttez les quenelles avec une écumoire, posez-les quelques instants sur du papier absorbant, puis sur la sauce au persil. Servez sans tarder en décorant avec quelques feuilles de persil.

POUR UNE VARIANTE AU CERFEUIL

Pour varier les plaisirs, vous pouvez remplacer le persil par la même quantité de cerfeuil.

QUENELLES AU NOIR DE SEICHE, SAUCE AUX CHIPIRONS

Facile — Faible — Léger

POUR 4 PERSONNES
PRÉPARATION : 10 MIN
CUISSON : 30 MIN
CONSERVATION : 48 H AU RÉFRIGÉRATEUR AVANT CUISSON

CRÈMERIE

Œufs : 2
Lait : 17 cl
Beurre : 70 g

POISSONNERIE

Chipirons : 200 g (poids net)

PRIMEUR

Ail : 2 gousses
Romarin frais : 1 branche

ÉPICERIE

Farine : 100 g
Pulpe de tomate : 1 boîte
Encre de seiche : 1 sachet (4 g)
Vin blanc sec : 1 verre
Huile d'olive : 3 c. à s.
Sel, poivre du moulin

Picpoul-de-pinet

1 PRÉPAREZ LES INGRÉDIENTS

Lavez les chipirons, puis égouttez-les et épongez-les soigneusement. Pelez et hachez les gousses d'ail. Hachez les feuilles de romarin.

2 CUISINEZ

Dans une casserole, faites bouillir le lait avec du sel et le beurre. Lorsque le beurre est fondu, retirez le récipient du feu et versez la farine en une seule fois. Mélangez à l'aide d'un fouet et remettez sur le feu pendant 5 minutes, sans cesser de mélanger. Quand la pâte se détache des parois, versez-la dans un saladier, ajoutez les œufs l'un après l'autre, l'encre de seiche et 1 gousse d'ail. Mélangez. En vous aidant de 2 cuillères, formez les quenelles comme expliqué dans la recette de base p. 6.

3 FAITES CUIRE

Faites pocher les quenelles dans 4 litres d'eau bouillante salée. Dès la reprise de l'ébullition, baissez le feu pour ne maintenir qu'un léger frémissement. Laissez cuire 15 minutes. Entre-temps, dans une poêle, versez l'huile, et faites-y revenir l'ail restant et le romarin. Ajoutez les chipirons, mélangez, puis versez le vin blanc et laissez-le s'évaporer. Mettez ensuite la pulpe de tomate, poivrez, salez, couvrez et laissez cuire 15 minutes environ. Puis ôtez la branche de romarin et réservez au chaud.

4 DRESSEZ

Égouttez les quenelles avec une écumoire et posez-les quelques instants sur du papier absorbant. Répartissez-les dans les assiettes, nappez-les avec la sauce aux chipirons et servez.

LA VARIANTE

Selon votre goût et/ou les disponibilités, vous pouvez remplacer les chipirons par des encornets.

QUENELLES AU SAFRAN, SAUCE AUX FRUITS DE MER

Facile   Moyen   Grande tablée

POUR 4 PERSONNES
PRÉPARATION : 10 MIN
CUISSON : 25 MIN
CONSERVATION : 48 H AU RÉFRIGÉRATEUR AVANT CUISSON

CRÈMERIE

Œufs : 2 moyens
Lait : 17 cl
Beurre : 70 g
Parmesan râpé : 2 c. à s.

POISSONNERIE

Fruits de mer (coques, moules) : 1,5 kg

PRIMEUR

Persil plat : 1 botte
Ail : 1 gousse

ÉPICERIE

Farine : 100 g
Safran : 1 dose
Huile d'olive : 8 c. à s.
Sel, poivre du moulin

Pouilly-fumé

1 PRÉPAREZ LES INGRÉDIENTS

Lavez et hachez les feuilles de persil. Épluchez la gousse d'ail. Grattez et lavez les moules. Plongez les coques dans de l'eau salée pour éliminer le sable.

2 CUISINEZ

Remplissez un faitout d'eau et mettez-la à bouillir. Dans une autre casserole, faites bouillir le lait avec du sel, du poivre et le beurre. Hors du feu, versez la farine en une fois, mélangez à l'aide d'un fouet et remettez sur le feu 5 minutes, sans cesser de mélanger. Quand la pâte se détache des parois, versez-la dans un récipient, ajoutez le safran, le parmesan et les œufs l'un après l'autre. En vous aidant de 2 cuillères, formez les quenelles comme expliqué dans la recette de base p. 6.

3 FAITES CUIRE

Faites pocher les quenelles dans 4 litres d'eau bouillante salée. Dès la reprise de l'ébullition, baissez le feu pour ne maintenir qu'un léger frémissement. Laissez cuire 12 minutes. Pendant ce temps, faites ouvrir les fruits de mer dans une poêle avec 2 cuillerées à soupe d'huile et la gousse d'ail. Puis éliminez l'ail, décoquillez les fruits de mer, filtrez leur jus (conservez-le à part) et réservez au chaud. Dans une large poêle, faites chauffer l'huile restante, ajoutez les fruits de mer avec 2 cuillerées à soupe de leur jus et le persil haché. Faites bouillir la sauce pendant 2 minutes.

4 DRESSEZ

Égouttez les quenelles et servez-les en portions avec leur sauce.

POUR UNE SAUCE AUX GAMBAS

Ces quenelles se marient très bien également avec cette sauce délicieuse : faites revenir 500 g de gambas dans 3 cuillerées à soupe d'huile d'olive extra-vierge, avec 1 gousse d'ail et du persil haché.

QUENELLES AU SAUMON FUMÉ ET SA CRÈME AUX BAIES DE CORIANDRE

Facile Moyen Fête

POUR 4 PERSONNES
PRÉPARATION : 10 MIN
CUISSON : 15 MIN
CONSERVATION : 48 H AU RÉFRIGÉRATEUR AVANT CUISSON

RAYON FRAIS

Saumon fumé : 300 g

CRÈMERIE

Crème fleurette : 23 cl
Œuf : 1 jaune

PRIMEUR

Échalote : 1
Baies de coriandre : ½ c. à s.

ÉPICERIE

Vin : 50 cl
Sel, poivre du moulin

Jurançon

1 PRÉPAREZ LES INGRÉDIENTS

Pelez et coupez l'échalote en deux. Concassez grossièrement les baies de coriandre.

2 CUISINEZ

Préparez les quenelles : passez le saumon au mixeur avec 13 cl de crème, le jaune d'œuf et du poivre. Préparez la sauce : dans une casserole, faites réduire de moitié, sur feu vif, le vin avec l'échalote, la coriandre concassée, du sel et du poivre. Ajoutez 10 cl de crème et laissez bouillir à feu doux jusqu'à l'obtention d'une sauce sirupeuse. Filtrez et gardez au chaud. En vous aidant de 2 cuillères, formez les quenelles comme expliqué dans la recette de base p. 6.

3 FAITES CUIRE

Faites pocher les quenelles dans 4 litres d'eau bouillante salée. Dès la reprise de l'ébullition, baissez le feu pour ne maintenir qu'un léger frémissement. Laissez cuire 3 minutes.

4 DRESSEZ

Répartissez les quenelles dans les assiettes, nappez-les de sauce chaude et servez.

POUR UN GOÛT PLUS DÉLICAT

Vous pouvez remplacer le saumon fumé par du saumon frais.

QUENELLES AUX CHÂTAIGNES, SAUCE AUX PÉTONCLES ET AU MARTINI

Facile · Faible · Végétarien

POUR 4 PERSONNES
PRÉPARATION : 10 MIN
CUISSON : 25 MIN
CONSERVATION : 48 H AU RÉFRIGÉRATEUR AVANT CUISSON

CRÈMERIE

Œufs : 2
Lait : 12,5 cl
Crème fleurette : 12,5 cl
Beurre : 50 g
Parmesan : 30 g

POISSONNERIE

Pétoncles : 250 g (poids net)

PRIMEUR

Échalote : 1

ÉPICERIE

Farine de châtaigne : 25 g
Farine de blé : 50 g
Noix muscade : 1 pincée
Martini bianco : 2 cl
Huile d'olive extra-vierge : 1 c. à s.
Sel, poivre du moulin

1 PRÉPAREZ LES INGRÉDIENTS

Râpez le parmesan. Pelez et hachez l'échalote.

2 CUISINEZ

Dans une casserole, faites bouillir le lait avec du sel, puis ajoutez le beurre. Lorsque le beurre est fondu, retirez le récipient du feu et versez les farines en une fois. Mélangez à l'aide d'un fouet et remettez sur le feu 5 minutes, sans cesser de mélanger. Quand la pâte se détache des parois, versez-la dans un récipient et ajoutez les œufs l'un après l'autre, la muscade et le parmesan. En vous aidant de 2 cuillères, formez les quenelles comme expliqué dans la recette de base p. 6.

3 FAITES CUIRE

Faites pocher les quenelles dans 4 litres d'eau bouillante salée. Dès la reprise de l'ébullition, baissez le feu pour ne maintenir qu'un léger frémissement. Laissez cuire 12 minutes. Pendant ce temps, faites revenir l'échalote dans l'huile, ajoutez les pétoncles et laissez cuire 2 minutes de chaque côté. Puis salez et poivrez, montez le feu, versez le Martini et faites flamber. Ajoutez la crème, mélangez et gardez au chaud.

4 DRESSEZ

Égouttez les quenelles avec une écumoire et posez-les quelques instants sur du papier absorbant, puis sur un plat de service. Nappez avec la sauce aux pétoncles et servez.

POUR UNE SAUCE AUX HERBES FRAÎCHES ET AU FROMAGE

Vous pouvez accompagner ces quenelles d'une autre sauce : faites revenir, dans 30 g de beurre, 6 feuilles de sauge, les feuilles de ½ bouquet de persil plat haché et celles de 2 tiges de romarin haché. Ajoutez 150 g de fromage à raclette de bonne qualité coupé en petits dés et laissez fondre.

QUENELLES RICOTTA ET CHOCOLAT

Facile — Faible — Fête

POUR 4 PERSONNES
PRÉPARATION : 20 MIN
CUISSON : 5 MIN
CONGÉLATION : 30 MIN
CONSERVATION : 48 H AU RÉFRIGÉRATEUR AVANT CUISSON

CRÈMERIE

Ricotta : 500 g

PRIMEUR

Framboises : 200 g

ÉPICERIE

Gélatine : 8 g
Raisins secs : 40 g
Chocolat noir : 50 g
Sucre : 65 g

1 PRÉPARER LES INGRÉDIENTS

Faites ramollir la gélatine dans un bol d'eau froide. Puis essorez-la. Concassez grossièrement le chocolat.

2 CUISINEZ

Dans une casserole, faites fondre 50 g de sucre avec 1 cuillerée à soupe d'eau. Ajoutez la gélatine essorée, faites-la dissoudre en mélangeant et versez cette préparation sur la ricotta. Ajoutez le chocolat, les raisins secs et le sucre restant. En vous aidant de 2 cuillères, formez les quenelles comme expliqué dans la recette de base p. 6 et placez-les au congélateur 30 minutes. Mixez les framboises (sauf quelques-unes que vous utiliserez pour la décoration).

3 DRESSEZ

Distribuez la sauce aux framboises dans des assiettes de service. Posez sur chaque assiette 2 quenelles, décorez avec les framboises réservées et dégustez sans attendre.

POUR UNE NOTE ACIDULÉE ET SUCRÉE

Vous pouvez remplacer les raisins secs par la même quantité de fruits confits coupés en petits dés.

QUENELLES DE MERINGUE MOELLEUSE, SAUCE AUX PÊCHES

Facile — Faible — Fête

POUR 4 PERSONNES
PRÉPARATION : 10 MIN
CUISSON : 5 MIN
CONSERVATION : 48 H AU RÉFRIGÉRATEUR AVANT CUISSON

CRÈMERIE

Œufs : 100 g de blancs exactement (soit 2 blancs environ)

Lait : 20 cl

PRIMEUR

Menthe : 1 belle poignée de feuilles

Citron : 1

ÉPICERIE

Pêches au sirop : 1 boîte (400 g environ)

Sucre : 100 g

Pignons : 20 g

1 PRÉPAREZ LES INGRÉDIENTS

Égouttez les pêches. Lavez les feuilles de menthe. Lavez le citron, prélevez et râpez le zeste. Dans une poêle antiadhésive sans matière grasse, faites griller les pignons en les mélangeant sans arrêt.

2 CUISINEZ

Mixez les pêches avec la menthe et le zeste de citron. Réservez. Montez les blancs d'œufs en neige ferme avec le sucre. En vous aidant de 2 cuillères, formez les quenelles comme expliqué dans la recette de base p. 6.

3 FAITES CUIRE

Portez le lait à ébullition avec 10 cl d'eau. Laissez cuire les quenelles 40 secondes de chaque côté à feu très doux.

4 DRESSEZ

Égouttez soigneusement les quenelles avec une écumoire et disposez-les dans les assiettes. Distribuez la sauce aux pêches sur les quenelles, décorez avec les pignons et servez.

LA VARIANTE AMARETTI

Pour une saveur délicatement amère et aux senteurs d'amande, vous pouvez remplacer les pignons par une dizaine de biscuits amaretti émiettés.

QUENELLES DE MARRONS ET PISTACHES

Facile Moyen Express

POUR 4 PERSONNES
PRÉPARATION : 15 MIN
CUISSON : 10 MIN
CONGÉLATION : 20 MIN
CONSERVATION : 48 H AU RÉFRIGÉRATEUR AVANT CUISSON

ÉPICERIE

Crème de marrons : 300 g
Pistaches non salées : 160 g
Chocolat noir : 80 g

1 **PRÉPAREZ LES INGRÉDIENTS**
Hachez les pistaches grossièrement. Cassez le chocolat dans un saladier.

2 **FAITES CUIRE**
Faites fondre le chocolat au bain-marie, puis laissez-le tiédir.

3 **ASSEMBLEZ**
Dans un autre saladier, mélangez la crème de marrons, 130 g de pistaches et le chocolat fondu. En vous aidant de 2 cuillères, formez les quenelles comme expliqué dans la recette de base p. 6, puis laissez figer au congélateur pendant 20 minutes.

4 **DRESSEZ**
Servez en portions et décorez avec les pistaches réservées.

À RÉSERVER AUX ADULTES

Pour une recette plus méditerranéenne, vous pouvez ajouter à la préparation 2 cuillerées à soupe de rhum et remplacer les pistaches décoratives sur les quenelles par de la gélatine de mandarine en nappage.

QUENELLES DE CHOCOLAT AU SABAYON

Moyenne — Faible — Grande tablée

POUR 4 PERSONNES
PRÉPARATION : 15 MIN
CUISSON : 15 MIN
RÉFRIGÉRATION : 5 H
CONSERVATION : 48 H AU RÉFRIGÉRATEUR AVANT CUISSON

CRÈMERIE

Œufs : 3 jaunes
Lait : 30 cl

ÉPICERIE

Chocolat à 70 % de cacao : 100 g
Gélatine : 2 g
Sucre : 60 g
Biscuits amaretti : 65 g
Marsala : l'équivalent de 2 demi-coques d'œufs

1 PRÉPAREZ LES INGRÉDIENTS

Faites ramollir la gélatine dans un bol d'eau froide. Puis essorez-la. Hachez le chocolat et les amaretti séparément.

2 CUISINEZ

Fouettez 2 jaunes d'œufs avec 30 g de sucre. Ajoutez le lait froid peu à peu, sans cesser de fouetter. Transférez la préparation dans une casserole avec le chocolat haché et faites chauffer doucement ; la crème ne doit pas bouillir. Ajoutez la gélatine essorée, les amaretti hachés, puis mélangez délicatement. Laissez refroidir au réfrigérateur pendant 5 heures (ou une nuit entière). À la sortie du réfrigérateur, en vous aidant de 2 cuillères, formez les quenelles comme expliqué dans la recette de base p. 6. Dans le même temps, préparez un bain-marie frémissant. Dans un saladier, fouettez ensemble le jaune d'œuf et le sucre restants, puis incorporez le marsala en deux fois.

3 FAITES CUIRE

Posez le saladier dans le bain-marie et continuez à fouetter jusqu'à ce que la préparation ait triplé de volume. Retirez le saladier du bain-marie et continuez à fouetter jusqu'au refroidissement complet.

4 DRESSEZ

Répartissez les quenelles dans les assiettes de service, nappez-les de sabayon et servez.

POUR UN GOÛT NOISETTE

Vous pouvez remplacer les amaretti par la même quantité de praliné.

LE SAVIEZ-VOUS ?

- Le mot « quenelle » est issu de l'allemand « Knödel » ou « Knoffle », qui signifie « boule de pâte ».
- Selon Apicius, le célèbre gastronome romain du Ier siècle avant J.-C. et auteur de *L'Art culinaire*, ses contemporains préparaient des recettes à base de crustacés ou de coquillages pilés au mortier, auxquels ils ajoutaient des condiments (du poivre et une sauce de poisson appelée *garum*). Ils complétaient avec des œufs, de la farine et du lait. Puis cette pâte était cuite dans de l'eau bouillante.
- Les quenelles étaient également dégustées à la cour du roi Louis XV où elles étaient considérées comme un mets raffiné. Les cuisiniers de l'époque eurent alors l'idée d'en faire un plat « noble » en lui adjoignant une farce de poisson ou de gibier.
- D'après Félix Benoit (*La Cuisine des Traboules*, éditions Solar, 1983), la quenelle lyonnaise apparut dans les années 1830 et faisait partie des repas de fêtes. Et parce que la Saône abritait une grande quantité de brochets, un maître pâtissier, Charles Morateur, eut l'idée d'incorporer la chair de ce poisson dans une pâte à choux.
- À Nantua, la quenelle a toujours été fabriquée avec 22 % de chair noble au minimum.

ÉQUIVALENCES & MESURES

1 CUILL. À SOUPE =

15 g de sucre, farine, beurre

12 g de crème fraîche, huile

3 cl de liquide

3 cuill. à café

1 CUILL. À CAFÉ =

5 g de sel, huile, sucre, farine

7 g de beurre

0,5 cl de liquide

1 NOISETTE DE BEURRE = 4 g

1 PINCÉE DE SEL = 3 à 5 g

1 MORCEAU DE SUCRE = 5 g

TEMPÉRATURES DU FOUR

Th. 3 = 90 °C

Th. 4 = 120 °C

Th. 5 = 150 °C

Th. 6 = 180 °C

Th. 7 = 210 °C

Th. 8 = 240 °C

ASSOCIATIONS DE SAVEURS

	MEILLEURS ACCORDS SALÉS	ACCORDS SUCRÉS	ET POURQUOI PAS ?
Aneth	Poissons blancs, concombre		Fromage blanc, yaourt
Basilic	Légumes méditerranéens, volailles, poissons blancs		Fraises
Ciboulette	Poissons, viandes blanches et volailles, salades, sauces crémées et vinaigrettes		Fromage blanc, yaourts (sauces)
Citronnelle	Poissons blancs et fruits de mer, plats et salades asiatiques		Champignons
Coriandre (feuilles)	Plats moyen-orientaux, mexicains et asiatiques, yaourts (sauces), salades		Mangue, orange, ananas
Estragon	Volailles et viandes blanches, œufs, sauces		
Menthe	Agneau, petits pois, salades, boulgour, yaourts (et sauces)	Pêches, fraises, melon	Chocolat (noir ou blanc)
Romarin	Lapin, poulet, pommes de terre		Pains et gâteaux, fruits jaunes rôtis ou pochés
Sauge	Veau, porc, volailles, foie, plats italiens		Salades de fruits
Thym	Viandes et volailles en cocotte ou rôties, pommes de terre		Fruits cuits, pochés ou en salade (sirop)
Badiane	Plats asiatiques	Banane (compote)	Pêches, cerises (cuites ou pochées)
Cannelle	Agneau, plats moyen-orientaux, mexicains et indiens	Pomme, poire, riz au lait, crèmes, fruits cuits ou pochés	Oranges en salade Cakes et gâteaux
Coriandre (grains)	Légumes (à la grecque), plats moyen-orientaux et indiens	Pains et gâteaux	
Cumin	Agneau, tajines, couscous, carottes, chou-fleur, haricots, plats mexicains		Abricots, mangue, pain, fromages
Girofle	Porc, bœuf poché ou braisé, béchamel		Pommes ou pêches cuites (crumble)
Paprika	Plats moyen-orientaux et d'Europe de l'Est, pommes de terre, haricots blancs, veau		Fromage frais
Piment, piment d'Espelette	Volailles, viandes blanches, porc, pommes de terre, haricots rouges, avocat, fruits de mer		Ananas, œufs
Poivres	Viandes rouges (noir), poissons (vert et baies roses)		Poires, fraises, sorbets
Safran	Poissons blancs, crustacés, moules, risotto, plats moyen-orientaux		Pêches, crèmes sucrées
Sésame	Viandes blanches, poissons blancs, crustacés, salades asiatiques	Pains et gâteaux	Caramel, miel
Vanille		Coulis, sauces, crèmes, glaces, compotes	Homard, poissons blancs

La recette de l'invité prestige

LA MAISON GIRAUDET

WOK DE QUENELLES, LÉGUMES ET GAMBAS

POUR 4 PERSONNES
PRÉPARATION : 15 MIN
CUISSON : 12 MIN

FAIT MAISON

Quenelles de brochet : 4 de 80 g chacune (voir recette p. 6 ou au rayon épicerie)

POISSONNERIE

Gambas : 16

PRIMEUR

Pois gourmands : 100 g

Carottes fanes : 2

Courgette : 1

Patate douce : 1

Oignon rouge : 1

Gingembre frais haché : 1 c. à s.

Coriandre fraîche : quelques feuilles

ÉPICERIE

Sauce soja : quelques gouttes

Piment de Cayenne : 3 pincées

Huile d'olive : 5 cl

1 PRÉPARAREZ LES INGRÉDIENTS

Épluchez et émincez l'oignon, la courgette et les carottes finement. Épluchez et découpez la patate douce en petits dés. Coupez les quenelles en rondelles.

2 CUISINEZ

Faites chauffer le wok et versez-y la moitié de l'huile d'olive. Faites revenir vivement l'oignon avec les gambas et la patate douce pendant 5 minutes, puis retirez le tout. Versez le reste d'huile dans la poêle et faites revenir les carottes, la courgette et les pois gourmands pendant 4 minutes environ. Ajoutez les quenelles et le gingembre, et assaisonnez de piment et de sauce soja. Réunissez tous les légumes dans le wok et faites sauter vivement encore 2 minutes.

3 DRESSEZ

Parsemez de coriandre fraîche et servez très chaud.

GIRAUDET

www.giraudet.fr

Spécialiste de la quenelle depuis plus de 100 ans, la maison Giraudet propose, dans ses boutiques et dans son bar à soupes et à quenelles, des produits artisanaux frais, naturels et savoureux